Four Seasons of Quilts

Four Seasons of Quilts

GARDEN-INSPIRED PROJECTS

CORI DERKSEN

MYRA HARDER

Martingale®
& COMPANY

Four Seasons of Quilts: Garden-Inspired Projects
© 2003 by Cori Derksen and Myra Harder

 That Patchwork Place®

That Patchwork Place® is an imprint
of Martingale & Company®.

Martingale & Company
20205 144th Avenue NE
Woodinville, WA 98072-8478
www.martingale-pub.com

Printed in China
08 07 06 05 04 03   8 7 6 5 4 3 2 1

Library of Congress Cataloging-in-Publication Data
Derksen, Cori.
   Four seasons of quilts / Cori Derksen and Myra
Harder.
      p. cm.
   ISBN 1-56477-481-3
   1. Patchwork—Patterns. 2. Appliqué—Patterns.
3. Quilting. 4. Gardens in art. I. Harder, Myra. II. Title.
   TT835 .D4635 2003
   746 .46'041—dc22
                                        2003016709

❖ **Mission Statement** ❖
Dedicated to providing quality products
and service to inspire creativity.

❖ *Credits* ❖

President ❖ Nancy J. Martin
CEO ❖ Daniel J. Martin
Publisher ❖ Jane Hamada
Editorial Director ❖ Mary V. Green
Managing Editor ❖ Tina Cook
Technical Editor ❖ Ellen Pahl
Copy Editor ❖ Liz McGehee
Design Director ❖ Stan Green
Illustrator ❖ Robin Strobel
Cover and Text Designer ❖ Regina Girard
Photographer ❖ Brent Kane

Dedication

To Mothers and Daughters

*A daughter cannot truly understand her mother
until she herself becomes one.*

*Quilting can be easily compared to raising a child. You start with small pieces
of beautiful fabric and work hard at it and one day it becomes a beautiful
quilt. So, too, with raising children, you start with a small, beautiful
child and with a lot of love, nurturing, discipline, and the help of
God, that child grows into something even more beautiful.*

Acknowledgments

Our sincere thanks and appreciation go to:

❖ Our mothers and mothers-in-law: Cathy Braun and Alvina Derksen; Betty Klassen and Agatha Harder.

❖ Our families and friends who support and encourage us and put up with us at deadline time!

❖ Betty Klassen, Myra's mother who loves to garden and quilt. We thank her for quality control, for making us strive for perfection, and for constantly encouraging us. She always goes the extra mile for us, with extraordinary handwork, embroidery, hand quilting, and wonderful machine quilting, too. We also want to acknowledge her store, Quilter's Corner in Morden, Manitoba, for providing us with such a great fabric selection and helpful staff to work with.

❖ Pearl Braun-Dyck, or Lady Pearl as we call her. Her appliqué expertise is evident in the projects she completed for us. We want to thank her for her willingness and eagerness to appliqué our designs, and for all the "power appliquéing" she did to meet deadlines. She worked above and beyond the call of duty. Pearl is known for her extraordinary appliqué and for her quilt collection that includes an award-winning Baltimore Album quilt.

❖ Andrea Fehr, a longtime friend. We both went to school with her, and we always call Andrea when we want something pieced with precision. Andrea is also the first Canadian fabric designer for Moda. You may see her name on the selvage of Moda's fabrics.

❖ Jackie Pohl, who owns a machine quilting business, the Vintage Quiltery, in Gladestone, Manitoba. We thank her for always fitting us into her busy schedule and for machine quilting "How Does Your Garden Grow?"

❖ Marlene Lindal, our wonderful photographer.

❖ Special thanks to Martingale and Company for believing in our ideas and for transforming them into such beautiful books.

Contents

Introduction

You are cordially invited to a garden party!

Welcome to *Four Seasons of Quilts,* a garden party for every time of year! The idea came about with the drawing of the quilt "Butterfly Blue," and a garden theme slowly evolved from there.

Myra has a passion for antique quilts, those that involved many months of work and became an heirloom passed down through generations. Because of this, many of the quilts in this book feature handwork such as appliqué, embroidery, and hand quilting. If you choose to do all of this work by hand, the quilts are not necessarily quick to make. You can certainly speed up the process with quick appliqué methods and machine quilting, but we hope that you will enjoy the time needed to create some future heirlooms. We want to encourage quilters not to forget these time-honored principles of quilting. We also wanted to produce

patterns that would be at the level of our local quilters. We live in a rural farming community in southern Manitoba. In this area, if you are not a farmer, you are related to at least one! Many of the gifted quilters here live on farms where they take care of large vegetable gardens, flower patches, and hundreds of acres of crops in addition to their families. And somewhere in their spare time they produce beautiful quilts. Their workmanship is superb, and we hope that these designs will be up to their standards.

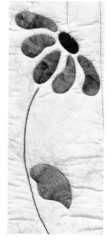

One could say that this book was inspired by our mothers. Our mothers and our mothers-in-law love to garden in one form or another. Whether it be a flower or a vegetable garden, they all enjoy puttering around in them. Thanks to our "moms" we have beautiful gardens to enjoy, as well as fresh vegetables to eat.

Our young children also spend time in the gardens, helping and learning along the way. Cori's daughter, Kierra, loves nothing more than to plant a seed or a flower and call it her own, and her son Lane's favorite thing is to feel the dirt between his fingers. Myra's son, Sam, loves to dig holes and drop in the seed, but he still thinks it's

wrong to cover up the seed with dirt. We hope that our children will be able to spend many enjoyable summer days in gardens.

This book has been fun for us. We love gardening, and this book shows a side of us that not many people know. We are known for color choices that are usually *not* pastel pink, blue, or lavender. With this book, we stepped out of our "box" to create different designs using different colors. Playing with color is something that we love to do, and working together, even though we think alike much of the time, can bring some very different combinations to our drawing table. The fact that we both have little girls now had a part to play in our color choices, too.

This brings us to the baby quilts. These are not typical baby quilts; we wanted to present quilts that could symbolize the season in which a child was born. The quilts can grow with the child or even be used as table toppers or wall hangings. We encourage you to think outside the box as we did; things do not always have to be used as they were originally intended.

As the seasons change, so can the quilts in your home. This book provides you with many opportunities to bring the outdoors in as the seasons change. We love changing and rearranging items in a room and love to use quilts in our decorating. The quilts in this book are perfect for rotating with the seasons.

The "signs," as we call them, are simple quilts that remind us of the seasons. Each of these is attached to wooden stretcher bars to give it the look of a piece of wall art. This is another great way to reflect the change of seasons in your home. Hang a sign in your front entry area or on a blank wall in the hallway.

Whether you are inspired by gardening or by quilting, this book will allow you to share your creativity with the loved ones around you, and hopefully that includes a mother

or a daughter. We hope that we have inspired you as much as our mothers and daughters have inspired us!

Cori and Myra

Getting Started

Our instructions assume that you are familiar with basic quiltmaking techniques, such as rotary cutting, and that you have some experience with piecing. It's important to cut accurately, piece with a precise ¼" seam, and press each seam after sewing. We've included some tips on choosing fabrics, instructions for paper foundation piecing and our favorite appliqué methods, and information on finishing your quilts.

FABRIC CHOICES

Cotton fabrics are the number one choice for quiltmaking. Cotton fabric is easy to work with and presses well. It has been proven that cotton quilts will last for many generations. If you use quality materials and stitch your quilt with care, many people will be able to enjoy your work for years to come.

Making color choices for these projects was sometimes a challenge, because we deviated from our normal palette of country colors. We used some beautiful Bali batiks for a number of different projects: "Butterfly Blue," "Dragonfly Baby Quilt," and in most of the "signs." The colors in the batiks are unique and beautiful; the shading lends itself very nicely to "fussy cutting" appliqué shapes to get a natural look.

We encourage you to change the colorways of the projects to suit your own taste, style, or decor. Changing colors may transform a project into your own masterpiece. Working at a quilt shop (Quilter's Corner, owned by Myra's mother, Betty Klassen) gives us firsthand experience helping quilters choose fabrics. This is further inspiration for us, motivating us to "step outside the box" and use colors that we normally wouldn't choose. Be creative, be daring, and don't get caught in a color rut!

SUPPLIES

Here are the essential items you'll need for making any of the projects in this book.

- ❖ Fabric and thread
- ❖ Paper for paper piecing (not all the quilt projects have paper-pieced blocks)
- ❖ Size 90/14 needles for paper piecing
- ❖ Freezer paper for appliqué
- ❖ Appliqué needles
- ❖ Iron
- ❖ Fabric scissors
- ❖ Rotary cutter
- ❖ Rotary-cutting ruler and mat
- ❖ Quilting needles
- ❖ Quilting thread
- ❖ Embroidery needles
- ❖ Embroidery floss

PAPER PIECING

Paper piecing is used in "How Does Your Garden Grow?" "Petunia Picnic," "Autumn Joy," and "Holly and Berries Table Runner." It's a good technique to use when you have intricate piecing, sharp points, or unusual shapes and sizes. You simply follow the numbers, sew on the lines, and your blocks will come out perfect. There are papers available specifically for paper-foundation piecing, but you can also use any paper that is easy to see through and tears away easily.

1. Transfer the pattern onto your paper foundation. Cut out the block along the dark solid line that runs around the outer edges. Cut multiple-unit blocks apart along each dark, solid line. Keep in mind that the pattern is the finished size of the block, so the fabric pieces need to extend at least ¼" beyond the edges of the paper foundation for the seam allowance.

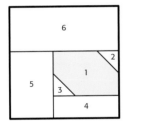
Single-unit block

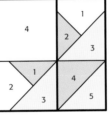
Multiple-unit block

2. Set the stitch length on your sewing machine for 15 to 18 stitches per inch. Insert a 90/14 needle into the machine. If you find that the paper tears away as you sew, decrease the number of stitches per inch; if the stitches loosen up when you pull the paper foundation away, increase the number of stitches per inch. It isn't necessary to backstitch, because the closeness of the stitches keeps the pieces from pulling apart.

3. Place each unit of the pattern in front of you with the marked side facing up. This will be referred to as the right side. The unmarked side will be referred to as the wrong side.

4. Begin with one unit and cut a piece of fabric for the part marked #1. Be sure it is *at least* ¼" larger all the way around than the size of the part it will cover (½" total). Do not attempt to cut the fabric to size. Just be sure the fabric amply covers the part; any excess will be trimmed away later.

5. Hold the pattern unit up to a light with the printed side facing you. Place the wrong side of the #1 fabric piece on the wrong side of the pattern so it covers part #1. Temporarily pin the piece in place. When you hold the block up to the light, part #1 should be completely covered by the fabric with at least ¼" all around for seam allowances.

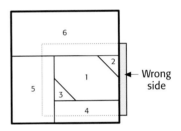
← Wrong side

6. Cut a piece of fabric for part #2. The fabric should be at least ¼" larger all the way around.

7. Hold the unit up to a light with the right side of the pattern facing you. Place fabric piece #2 over fabric piece #1, right sides together, with at least ¼" of fabric extending over the line that separates parts #1 and #2.

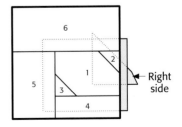
← Right side

8. Working on the right side of the pattern, sew on the thin black line that separates parts #1 and #2.

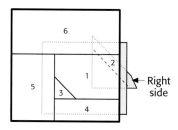

9. Fold back piece #2 along the seam line. Hold the unit up to the light. Be sure that parts #1 and #2 are covered and that the fabric piece for each part extends at least ¼" on all sides.

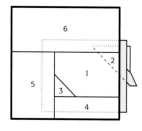

10. Working on the pattern's wrong side, fold piece #2 back so the wrong side of the fabric is facing up. Trim the seam allowance between parts #1 and #2 to ¼". If the excess fabric isn't trimmed away, it can build up and make quilting difficult later.

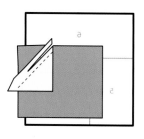

11. Fold piece #2 open. Finger-press or use a wooden pressing tool to press the seam allowance flat.

12. Continue adding fabric pieces, in numerical order, in the same manner for the remaining parts.

13. When you have added all of the fabric pieces to each block or unit, lightly press each block or unit and trim the outer seam allowances to ¼".

14. If you are piecing a multiple-unit block, stitch the units together. Remember that the finished block is a mirror image of the pattern. Lightly press the block.

15. Remove the paper foundation after all the edges have been sewn into another seam. This will keep the block stable until it is sewn into place.

Helpful Hints for Paper Piecing

Here are a few hints that we have learned along the way. We hope they will make paper piecing more enjoyable for you.

❖ Keep all threads trimmed short. They love to get caught in your machine and jam things up.

❖ If you use regular photocopy paper as a foundation, very lightly mist the paper with water before tearing if off. This makes it easier to remove and less likely to rip out your stitches.

❖ Always cut the largest pieces of fabric for your quilt first; then cut up the remaining fabric for piecing.

❖ Always press the completed units before joining them into blocks.

❖ Insert a pin along your intended sewing line on the right side of the pattern. Then when you turn your pattern over to lay down the next piece of fabric, you will have a seam-allowance guide to assist you in positioning the next piece of fabric.

BORDERS

Although specific border lengths are listed in the cutting directions for each project, it is best to measure your quilt top through the center in both directions before cutting the border strips for your quilt. For some of the quilts, we did not want the borders to be pieced, so you are instructed to cut the border strips on the lengthwise grain. You can cut border strips across the width of the fabric and piece as necessary if you prefer. This usually requires less fabric.

1. Measure the length of your quilt top through the center and cut two border strips to that measurement, piecing them if needed. Mark the centers of the strips and the centers along the side edges of the quilt. Pin the strips to the sides of the quilt, matching the centers and ends. Stitch in place. Press the seam allowances toward the borders.

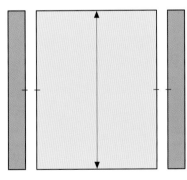

Measure center of quilt, top to bottom. Mark centers.

2. Measure the width of your quilt top through the center, including the side borders just added, and cut two border strips to that measurement, piecing as necessary. Mark the centers of the strips and the centers along the top and bottom edges of the quilt. Pin the strips to the top and bottom edges of the quilt, matching the centers and ends. Stitch in place. Press seam allowances toward the borders.

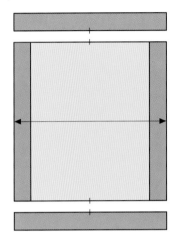

Measure center of quilt, side to side, including borders. Mark centers.

Cori's Party Hints

My four-year-old daughter and I like to host theme parties for our friends from time to time. We decorate a table and plan the menu around a theme, usually one based on an occasion or season. Displaying a quilt on a table is a great way to enhance your theme. "Webster's Tulips," "Petunia Picnic," and "Holly and Berries Table Runner" work well on tables. Even larger quilts such as "Autumn Joy" and "Christmas Goose" would be stunning arranged diagonally on a table. "Pumpkin Patch Baby Quilt" would make a sweet table topper for an autumn gathering.

APPLIQUÉ

There are many ways to do appliqué. We prefer a method that uses freezer paper. The freezer-paper template is pressed onto the right side of the fabric and used as a guide for turning the seam allowances under as you stitch the appliqué shape in place. Every new technique takes a little time to get used to, but we feel that once you have practiced this technique a few times, you will find it as easy and fast as we do. Follow these simple instructions.

1. Using a fine-line pencil, trace the appliqué pattern onto the background fabric. This gives you an accurate guide to follow when placing your appliqué shapes on the background blocks. It also ensures that all your blocks are exactly the same.

2. Use a fine-line pencil to trace the appliqué patterns onto the dull side of a piece of freezer paper.

3. Cut out each piece along the traced line. Do not leave any seam allowances around the appliqué templates.

4. Place the freezer-paper template on the right side of the appropriate fabric, shiny side down. Leave approximately ½" between pieces. Press the pieces in place with a hot iron.

5. Cut out each appliqué, leaving a ¼" allowance around each piece.

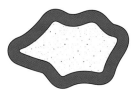

6. Place the appliqué on the background fabric, positioning it on the drawn lines. If needed, pin the appliqué in place, pinning through the middle of the piece so the edges are easily turned under for the appliqué.

7. Turn a portion of the seam allowance under until it is even with the edge of the freezer paper. Using a thread color that matches the appliqué piece, knot the end of the thread and secure it in the seam allowance. Insert the needle into the background fabric underneath the appliqué piece and come up through the background fabric about ⅛" away. With the tip of the needle, catch just the edge of the appliqué and pull the stitch taut. Continue this process until your piece is completely stitched into place.

8. Remove the freezer paper.

Appliquéing Curved Pieces

❖ On inside curves, make several clips slightly into the seam allowance (do not clip all the way to the stitching line); this will allow the fabric to spread and lie flat.

❖ Do not clip the seam allowance on outside curves.

❖ When appliquéing bias tubes or strips, always appliqué the concave curve first, then the convex.

Bias Tubes

When we make bias tubes for appliqué, we use bias press bars. They make it easy to stitch and press to get nice, even bias tubes.

1. Fold down a corner on the fabric you want to use, forming a triangle. The crosswise grain should meet the lengthwise grain of the

fabric. Mark along this fold. You will cut your bias strips along this line.

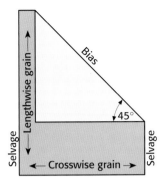

2. Using a ruler and rotary cutter, cut along the diagonal line to make your first cut. Measure from this cut edge and cut bias strips to the width specified in the project directions. Cut strips until you have the total length needed.

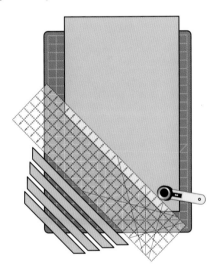

3. Fold the strip in half lengthwise, wrong sides together. Draw a seam line slightly wider than the width of the bias press bar you will use. This will be the finished width of your bias tube. For a ½" bias tube, draw the seam line slightly wider than ½".

4. Stitch along the drawn line and trim the excess seam allowance to ⅛" so it will be hidden behind the tube after pressing.

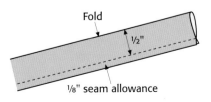

5. Insert the appropriate bias bar into the tube. Roll the seam allowance to the center of the flat side of the press bar. Press the seam in one direction, slipping the bar through the tube as you continue to press.

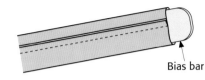

6. Remove the press bar and press the tube with a hot iron to hold the crease.

EMBROIDERY DETAILS

We have enhanced many of our patterns with the addition of a simple outline embroidery stitch. Use an embroidery hoop if desired.

1. Use two strands of embroidery floss for all the embellishing in this book. Cut lengths of embroidery thread approximately 18" long to avoid fraying and tangling thread.

2. Knot the end of your embroidery floss and bring the needle up through the fabric at point A and pull the thread taut. Insert the needle at point B and bring it up at point C, pulling the thread taut.

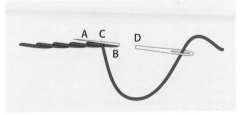

3. Insert the needle at point D, and continue stitching in this manner until you reach the end of your design line. You will work the stitch from left to right.

SPRING

Webster's Tulips

Appliquéd by Pearl Braun-Dyck; hand quilted by Pearl Braun-Dyck and Betty Klassen.

This square quilt was inspired by Marie Webster, a quilt designer in the early 1900s. Many of her quilts featured simple floral appliqué designs, and this Tulip quilt reflects her style.

I wanted to design a quilt that is classic and could pass for an antique. I also wanted it to have space to show off intricate quilting. Classic quilts with simple lines are timeless and have a universal appeal.

– Myra

Finished quilt: 58" x 58"
Finished block: 7" x 7"

MATERIALS

Yardage is based on 42"-wide fabric.

3¾ yards of off-white for background, borders 2 and 4, and binding

1⅝ yards of light green for leaves and borders 1 and 3 (or ⅔ yard of light green if you prefer to cut crosswise and piece the borders)

⅝ yard of medium green for stems

⅜ yard of dark yellow for tulips

¼ yard of medium yellow for tulips

3½ yards of fabric for backing

62" x 62" piece of batting

CUTTING

Note: When cutting the borders, you may want to add an extra inch and trim to size later.

From the lengthwise grain of the off-white fabric, cut:

❖ 2 strips, 1½" x 44½" (border 2 sides)
❖ 2 strips, 1½" x 46½" (border 2 top and bottom)
❖ 2 strips, 5½" x 48½" (border 4 sides)
❖ 2 strips, 5½" x 58½" (border 4 top and bottom)

From the remaining off-white fabric, cut:

❖ 36 squares, 8" x 8"
❖ 6 strips, 2½" x 42" (binding)

From the lengthwise grain of the light green fabric, cut:

❖ 2 strips, 1½" x 42½" (border 1 sides)
❖ 2 strips, 1½" x 44½" (border 1 top and bottom)
❖ 2 strips, 1½" x 46½" (border 3 sides)
❖ 2 strips, 1½" x 48½" (border 3 top and bottom)

From the medium green fabric, cut:

❖ 375" of 1¼"-wide bias strips

APPLIQUÉING THE BLOCKS

Refer to "Appliqué" on page 14 and "Embroidery Details" on page 15.

1. Trace the tulip appliqué pattern on page 21 onto the 8" background squares.

2. Prepare the stems from the bias strips, referring to "Bias Tubes" on page 14. The stems should finish at ³⁄₁₆". Prepare leaves and buds for freezer-paper appliqué.

3. Appliqué the shapes in place, starting with the stems, followed by the leaves and buds. Layer the petals as indicated in the pattern. Make 36 blocks. Trim and square the blocks to 7½" x 7½".

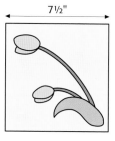

7½"

Make 36.

ASSEMBLING THE QUILT

1. Arrange the blocks in six rows of six blocks each, referring to the diagram for placement. You can arrange them to create a circular design as we did, or try the alternate setting option shown at right, creating more of a pinwheel look.

2. Sew the blocks together in rows. Press the seams in opposite directions from row to row.

3. Sew the rows together and press all the seams in the same direction.

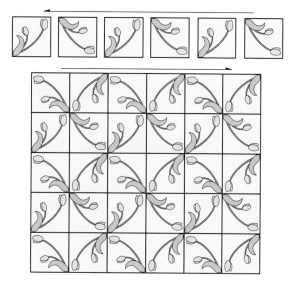

4. Refer to "Borders" on page 13. Measure through the center and add the borders in the appropriate order, referring to the quilt diagram.

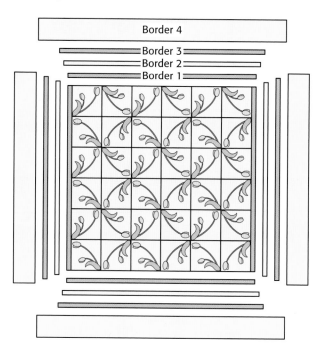

Border 4
Border 3
Border 2
Border 1

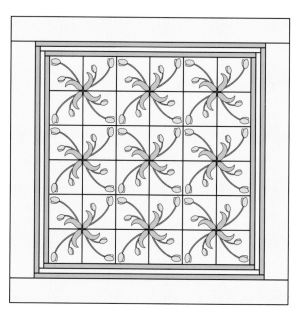

Alternate Setting

FINISHING THE QUILT

1. Cut the backing fabric into two equal pieces and sew them together side by side to make a backing that is at least 4" larger than your quilt top.

2. Layer the backing, batting, and quilt top; baste the layers together.

3. Quilt as desired. The quilt shown was hand quilted using a stencil design between the tulips, cross-hatching and a curved motif within the circular area, and feathers in the outer border.

4. Make and attach binding to your quilt, referring to "Binding" on page 92.

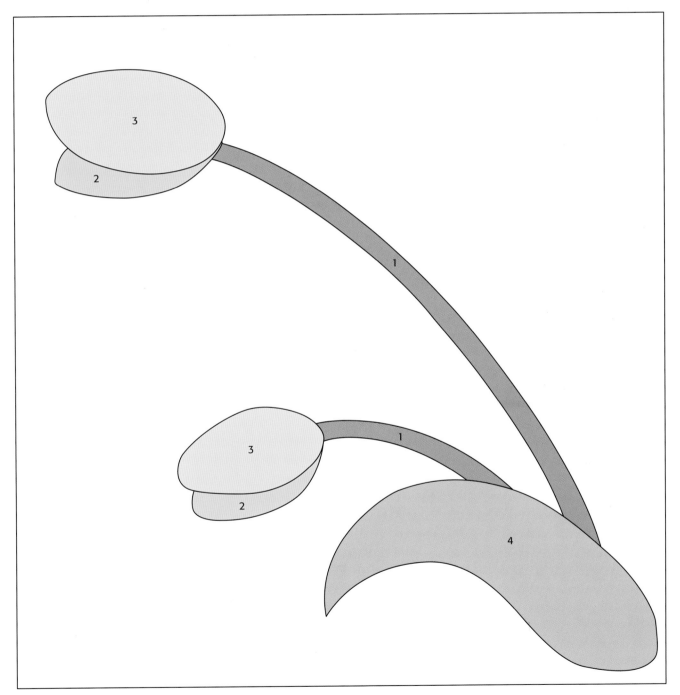

Tulip Appliqué Pattern

How Does
Your Garden Grow?

It has always been a joke that I have a pile of pink fabric in my stash, because it is just not me! However, my feelings about pink changed on Christmas Eve, when our beautiful daughter was born. Before I left the hospital, I was already thinking of all the pink quilts I wanted to make for her. This was one of the first designs that came to mind. I wanted a fun little girl's quilt with a touch of the 1930s look—the background and border had to be pink, of course!

– Myra

Myra usually leaves me in charge of naming our quilts. The fun, whimsical flowers reminded me of the children's nursery rhyme: "Mary, Mary, quite contrary, How does your garden grow? With silver bells and cockle shells and pretty maids all in a row."

– Cori

Finished quilt: 64" x 79"
Finished flower block: 5" x 5"

MATERIALS

Yardage is based on 42"-wide fabric.

2⅞ yards of small-scale pink floral for background, blocks, sashing, and border 1

2¼ yards of dark peach print for border 5 and binding (or 1¾ yards if you prefer to cut crosswise and piece your borders)

2⅛ yards of green print for leaves, stems, and borders 2 and 4 (or 1¼ yards if you prefer to cut crosswise and piece your borders)

1¾ yards of green stripe for border 3

¼ yard of orange for flowerpots

¼ yard *each* of 12 different colors for flowers (medium and dark blue, medium and dark rose, medium and dark pink, medium and dark teal, medium and dark purple, medium and dark lavender)

⅛ yard of yellow for flower centers

4 yards of fabric for backing

72" x 88" piece of batting

CUTTING

Note: When cutting the borders and sashing, you may want to add an extra inch and trim to size later.

From the lengthwise grain of the small-scale pink floral, cut:

❖ 4 strips, 3½" x 50½" (sashing and border 1 sides)

❖ 2 strips, 3½" x 45½" (border 1 top and bottom)

From the remaining small-scale pink floral, cut:

❖ 1 piece, 10½" x 11½"

❖ 1 piece, 5½" x 11½"

❖ 3 pieces, 4½" x 5½"

❖ 3 pieces, 2½" x 5½"

❖ 6 pieces, 1½" x 5½"

❖ 6 pieces, 1½" x 4½"

23

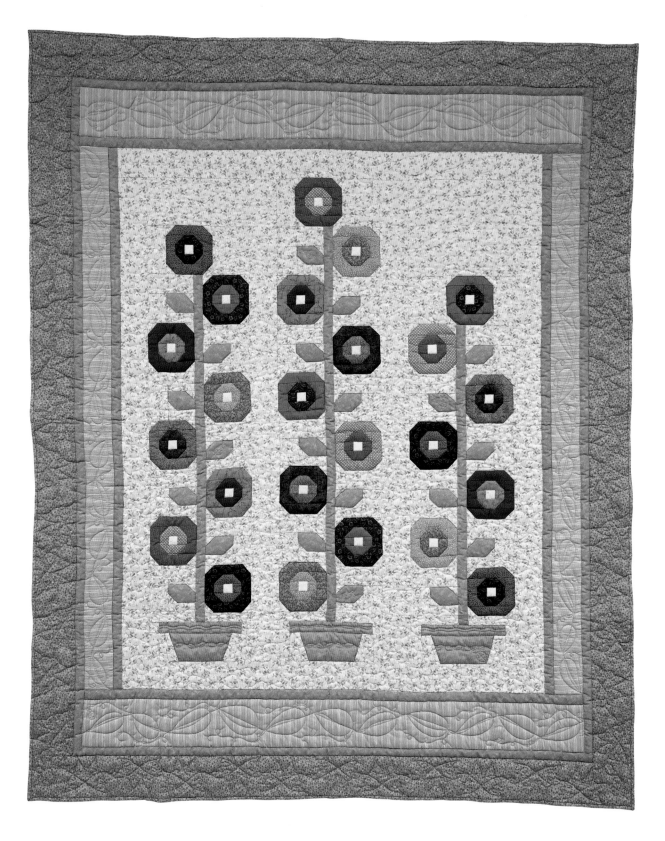

Pieced by Myra Harder; quilted by Jackie Pohl.

From the lengthwise grain of the green print, cut:

❖ 2 strips, 1½" x 56½" (border 2 sides)
❖ 2 strips, 1½" x 53½" (border 2 top and bottom)
❖ 2 strips, 1½" x 68½" (border 4 sides)
❖ 2 strips, 1½" x 55½" (border 4 top and bottom)
❖ 1 piece, 1½" x 40½"
❖ 1 piece, 1½" x 35½"
❖ 1 piece, 1½" x 30½"
❖ 3 squares, 1½" x 1½"

From the green stripe, cut:

❖ 3 strips, 3½" x 42" (border 3 sides)
❖ 3 strips, 5½" x 42" (border 3 top and bottom)

From the dark peach print, cut:

❖ 2 strips, 5" x 70½" (border 5 sides)
❖ 2 strips, 5" x 64½" (border 5 top and bottom)
❖ 8 strips, 2½" x 42" (binding)

To keep the flowers and leaves properly aligned, make alignment marks on the wrong side of each vine. Place a mark 5¼" from the top of each vine, and then mark every 5" below the first mark. When you join the rows to the vine, make sure that the blocks line up with the marks.

PIECING THE FLOWERS, LEAVES, AND POTS

Refer to "Paper Piecing" on page 11 for details as needed.

1. Make paper-piecing foundations from the patterns on pages 28–31. You will need 24 Flower blocks, 10 right leaves, 11 left leaves, and 3 pots. Remember, the leaves will be the mirror image of the pattern when they are completed.

2. Paper piece the blocks, making two of each flower-color combination as shown.

Make 10.

Make 11.

Make 2.

Make 2.

Make 2.

Make 2.

Make 2.

Make 2.

Make 2.

Make 2.

Make 2.

Make 2.

Make 3.

3. To complete the three pots, add a 1½" x 4½" background piece to each side of the Pot block. Join two 1½" x 5½" background pieces to each side of a 1½" green stem square. Add this to the top of the Pot block.

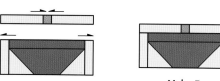

Make 3.

ASSEMBLING THE QUILT

1. To sew the first row (the left pot of flowers), alternate and sew together three Flower blocks and four left Leaf blocks. Press. Add this row to the left side of the 1½" x 35½" green print piece.

2. Sew another vertical row, alternating four Flower blocks and three right Leaf blocks. Add this row of flowers to the right side of the stem. Then add this unit to the top of a Pot block.

3. To finish the top of this row, make a unit of one Flower block and add the following background pieces. To the left side of the flower, add a 2½" x 5½" background piece. To the right side, add a 4½" x 5½" background piece, and to the top, add a 5½" x 11½" background piece. Sew the unit to the top of the row.

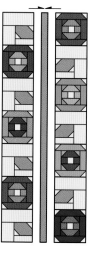

4. Piece the second pot row in the same order as the first, using eight Flower blocks, and four right and four left leaves. Use the 1½" x 40½" green stem piece. To make the top unit, add a 2½" x 5½" background piece to the left side of a Flower block, and add a 4½" x 5½" background piece to the right side. Sew the unit to the top of the row.

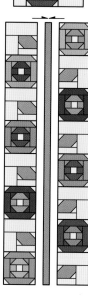

5. Piece the third pot row in the same order as the first two, using six Flower blocks, three right and three left leaves, and the 1½" x 30½" green stem piece. To make the top unit of this row, add a 4½" x 5½" background piece to the left side of a Flower block, add a 2½" x 5½" background piece to the right side, and add a 10½" x 11½" background piece to the top.

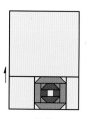
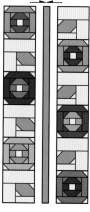

26

6. Join the three pot rows vertically, with a 3½" x 50½" sashing strip between each row. Press the seams toward the sashing strips.

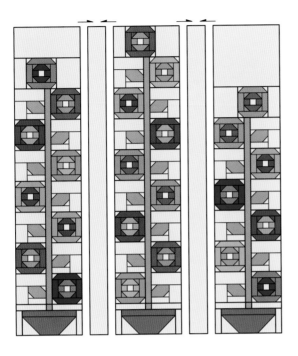

7. Referring to "Borders" on page 13, measure your quilt through the center and add border 1 to the sides, and then to the top and bottom. Press.

8. Add border 2 to the sides and press.

9. Piece the border 3 strips and cut to the length needed for your quilt. The stripes should be perpendicular to the quilt on all sides. Add border 3 to the sides.

10. Add borders 2 and 3 to the top and bottom. Press.

11. Add border 4 to the quilt and then border 5, pressing toward the border just added.

FINISHING THE QUILT

1. Cut the backing fabric into two equal pieces and sew them together side by side to make a backing that is at least 4" larger all around than your quilt top.

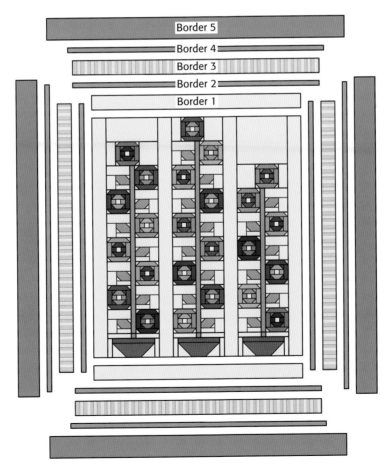

2. Layer the backing, batting, and quilt top; baste the layers together.

3. Quilt as desired. The quilt shown was machine quilted with a meandering stitch in the background. There are nine butterflies hidden throughout the pink background, and in the top right corner there are sunrays shining down. A leaf motif was quilted in the striped border, and in the outer border, a repeated butterfly pattern. If you look closely, you'll find 12 ladybugs hidden throughout the quilt, too!

4. Referring to "Binding" on page 92, make and attach binding to your quilt.

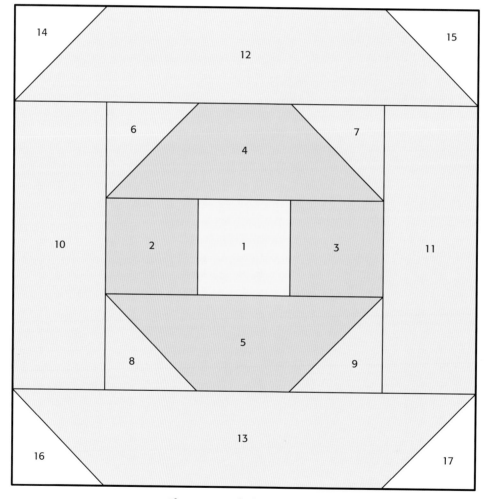

Flower Foundation Pattern
Make 24.

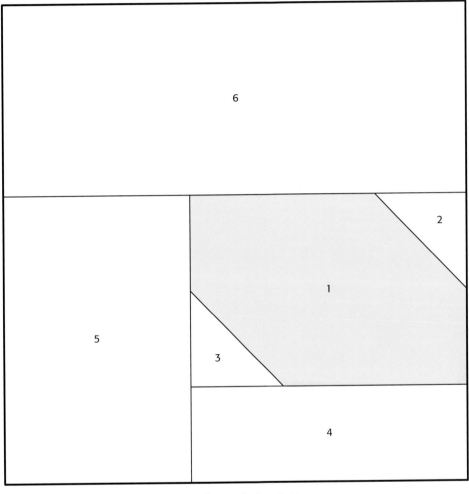

Right Leaf Foundation Pattern
Make 10.

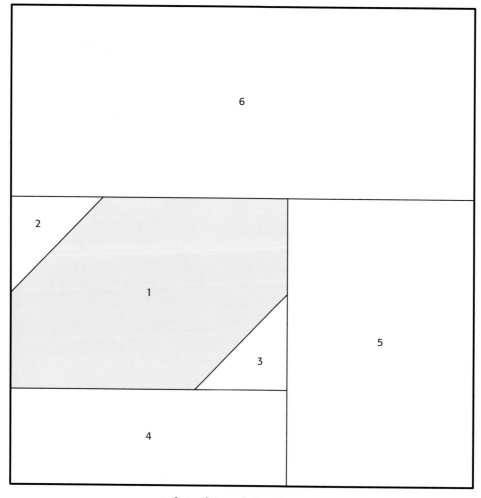

Left Leaf Foundation Pattern
Make 11.

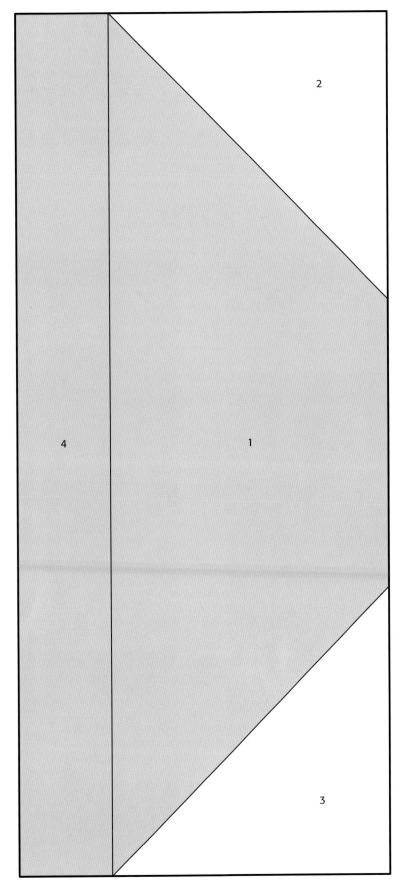

Pot Foundation Pattern
Make 3.

Signs of Spring

In Canada, the winters are very long, so when April rolls around I start to think of flowers. As soon as the snow melts, I check the gardens every day to see if anything is peeking through. The tulips are the first to pop up in my garden, and I delight in the fresh new color in the yard.

– Cori

Finished quilt: 14" x 9"

Appliquéd by Pearl Braun-Dyck; embroidered by Betty Klassen; hand quilted by Cori Derksen.

Materials

1 fat quarter of pale pink batik for background

1 fat quarter of green batik for stems and leaves

3" x 42" strip of medium pink batik for tulips

1 fat quarter of fabric for backing

18" x 22" piece of batting

Medium pink embroidery floss for *Spring*

2 pairs of stretcher bars, 9" and 14" long

Completing the Appliqué and Embroidery

Refer to "Appliqué" on page 14 and "Embroidery Details" on page 15.

1. Refer to "Bias Tubes" on page 14. Cut 36" of bias strips 1¼" wide from the green batik fat quarter. Using bias press bars, make ³⁄₁₆" bias tubes from the green bias strips.

2. Trace the pattern on pages 34 and 35 onto the center of the pink fat quarter.

3. Appliqué the stems first and then the leaves from right to left.

4. Appliqué the tulips, layering the petals as indicated on the pattern.

5. Embroider the word *Spring* in the lower-right corner.

Finishing the Sign

Refer to "Stretcher-Bar Framing" on page 94 to frame your "Signs of Spring."

Connect to pattern on page 35.

Connect to pattern on page 34.

SUMMER

Butterfly Blue

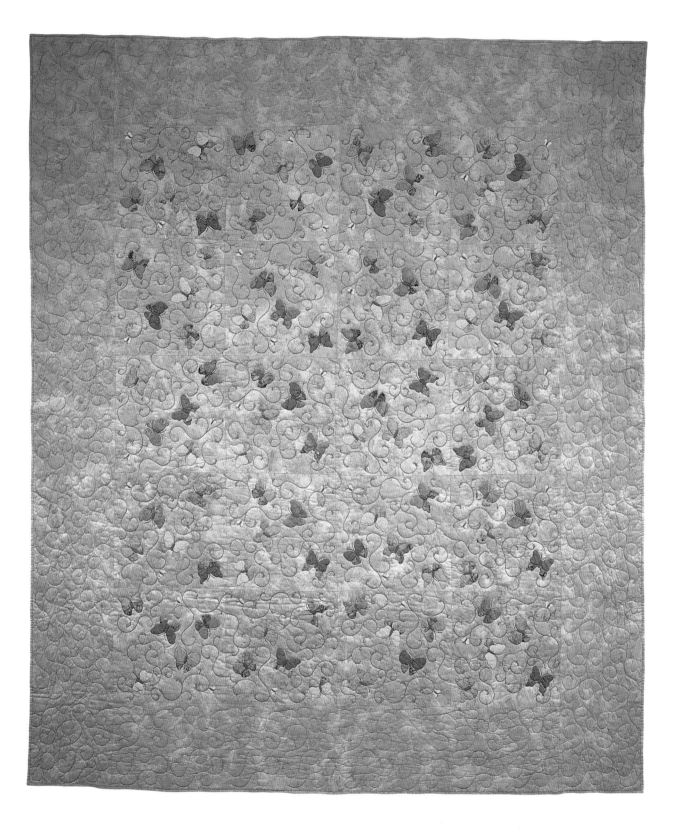

*Appliquéd by Pearl Braun-Dyck; embroidered by Betty Klassen;
quilted by the Glen Cross Church Ladies group.*

The design for this quilt came to me one night when I was lying in bed and couldn't sleep. I think I had been drawing butterflies that evening before I went to bed, because otherwise I don't know how that became the theme of the quilt! I wanted a quilt with an overall design that would showcase embroidery. I decided to break the quilt down into 16" blocks. Turning the blocks gives the illusion of butterflies swirling at random on a sunny summer day.

– Myra

Finished quilt: 88" x 104"

Finished block: 16" x 16"

MATERIALS

Yardage is based on 42"-wide fabric.

10½ yards of blue batik for background and binding

¾ yard of multicolored batik for lower wings of butterfly

¼ yard of dark blue for butterfly bodies

¼ yard *each* of 5 colors for upper wings of butterfly: pink, lavender, teal, rose, and plum

¼ yard of yellow for small butterfly wings

Scraps for small butterfly bodies

7¾ yards of fabric for backing

92" x 108" piece of batting

Embroidery floss:

15 skeins of light blue for swirls

2 skeins of dark blue for antennae

CUTTING

From the lengthwise grain of the blue batik, cut:

❖ 2 strips, 12½" x 80½"
❖ 2 strips, 12½" x 88½"

From the remainder of the blue batik, cut:

❖ 20 squares, 18" x 18"
❖ 10 strips, 2½" x 42" (binding)

COMPLETING THE APPLIQUÉ AND EMBROIDERY

Refer to "Appliqué" on page 14 and "Embroidery Details" on page 15.

1. Using the butterfly appliqué patterns on page 42 and the block diagram on page 40, make a master pattern on paper for butterfly placement and embroidery lines. Draw a 16" x 16" square to indicate the edges of the block. Trace the butterflies onto the paper, and then draw the curved embroidery lines. Draw them freehand or use a French curve to get smooth arcs.

2. Center and trace the pattern onto the 18" background squares.

3. Make appliqué templates for the five butterflies (A through E) and the small butterfly. You will need 16 of each large butterfly and 32 small butterflies.

4. From the multicolored print, cut all of the lower-wing pieces for the five different butterflies (16 pairs for each different butterfly). Appliqué each piece into position on the background fabric.

5. Choose the colors for the top wings according to the color of the bottom wings. We did not necessarily use each of the five colors in each block. Often we repeated wing colors, having two butterflies of the same color. Appliqué all of the top wings.

6. Appliqué the dark blue body onto all of the butterflies.

7. Appliqué the little yellow butterflies. Keep the wings together as one piece and then appliqué the body on top of the wing piece.

Embroidery Option

You can use embroidery thread and a satin stitch to make the small butterfly bodies if you prefer.

8. Embroider the antennae onto all of the butterflies.

9. Embroider the swirls on each block.

10. Press the blocks on the wrong side. Place the blocks on a cutting mat. Use a rotary cutter and a large square ruler to trim and square up your blocks to 16½" x 16½".

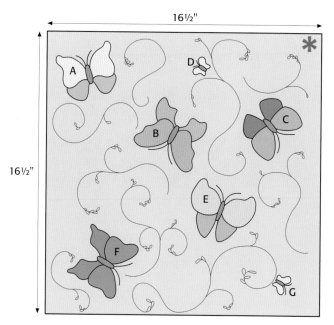

✳ Indicates orientation of block

Pressing Hint

Use a terry-cloth towel under your appliqué blocks when pressing. This will cushion the appliqués and the embroidery stitches to keep them from being flattened on the ironing surface.

ASSEMBLING THE QUILT

In the top right-hand corner of the block pattern, we have placed a mark (red asterisk). On each of our appliquéd blocks, we placed a pin where this mark is. If you want to match our block orientation, refer to the layout diagram. The dot on each block shows you how to rotate the block in the quilt layout.

1. Join the blocks into five horizontal rows. Press the seams in opposite directions from row to row. Sew the rows together. Press the seams all in one direction.

2. Refer to "Borders" on page 13. Add the 12½" x 80½" blue batik strips to the sides. Press toward the border. Sew the 12½" x 88" strips to the top and bottom. Press.

Embroidery Hint

When all of the blocks were joined, we added a few more embroidery swirls over the seams where we felt there was too large of an open area.

FINISHING THE QUILT

1. Cut the backing fabric into three equal pieces and sew them together to make a backing that is 4" larger than your quilt top.

2. Layer the backing, batting, and quilt top; baste the layers together.

3. Quilt as desired. The quilt shown was hand quilted by simply outlining the butterflies and following the blue embroidery swirls. In the border, the swirls were repeated with quilting stitches.

4. Referring to "Binding" on page 92, make and attach binding to your quilt.

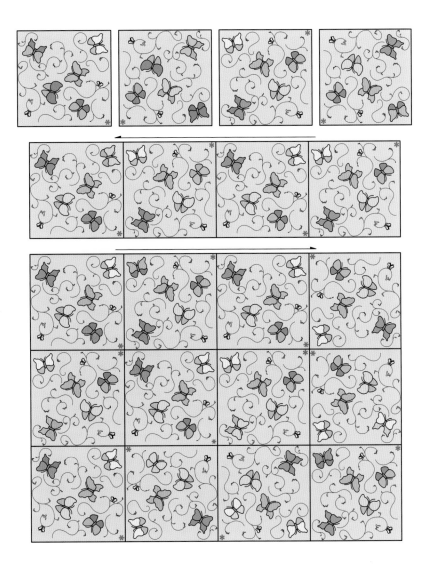

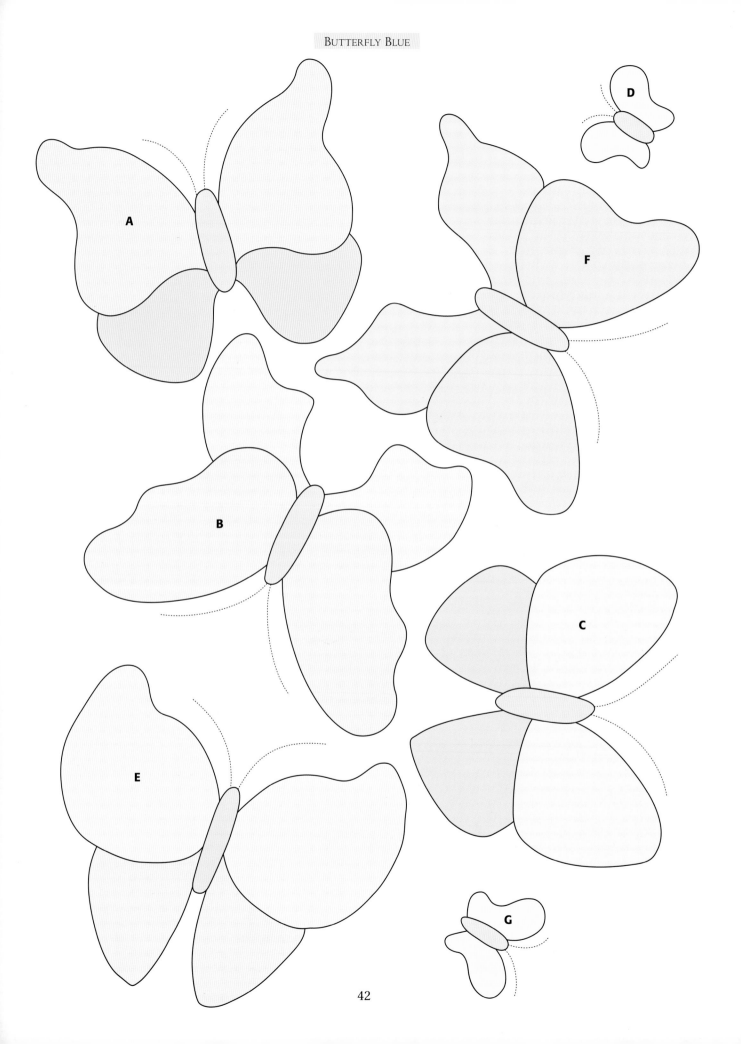

Petunia Picnic

Pieced by Cori Derksen; quilted by Betty Klassen.

The flowerlike pattern created by this modified version of the Storm at Sea block reminds me of a popular summer flower, the Wave petunia. The large plaid border makes me think of a picnic tablecloth, hence the name. I have many great memories of picnics with my children, and I hope this quilt inspires you to take time to make a few picnic memories of your own.

– Cori

Finished quilt: 56" x 56"

Finished bock: 7" x 7"

MATERIALS

Yardage is based on 42"-wide fabric.

2 yards of ivory for background and inner border

1¾ yards of plaid for outer border

⅝ yard of teal print for Flower blocks

⅜ yard of pink for Flower blocks

¼ yard of peach print for center of Flower blocks

⅛ yard of dark teal for blocks and corner squares

3½ yards of fabric for backing

⅝ yard of pink for binding

60" x 60" piece of batting

CUTTING

Note: You may want to wait until the center of the quilt is complete before cutting borders.

From the ivory background fabric, cut:

❖ 1 square, 17½" x 17½"
❖ 4 pieces, 3½" x 7½"
❖ 4 strips, 1½" x 17½"
❖ 2 strips, 1½" x 42"; crosscut into 8 pieces, 1½" x 7½"
❖ 2 strips, 2½" x 33½" (inner-border sides)
❖ 2 strips, 2½" x 37½" (inner-border top and bottom)

From the dark teal fabric, cut:

❖ 4 squares, 1½" x 1½"

From the lengthwise grain of the plaid fabric, cut:

❖ 2 strips, 10" x 37½" (outer-border sides)
❖ 2 strips, 10" x 56½" (outer-border top and bottom)

From the pink fabric for binding, cut:

❖ 6 strips, 2½" x 42"

PAPER PIECING THE BLOCKS

Referring to "Paper Piecing" on page 11, paper piece 12 Flower blocks, using the pattern on page 47.

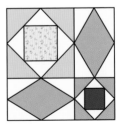

Make 12.

ASSEMBLING THE QUILT

1. To opposite sides of the 17½" center square, add a 1½" x 17½" ivory strip. Add a 1½" dark teal square to each end of the other two 1½" x 17½" ivory strips and sew these to the top and bottom of the center square.

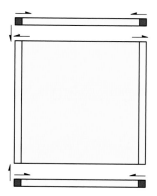

2. Join two Flower blocks with a 3½" x 7½" ivory piece between them. The flowers should face each other as shown. Add a 1½" x 7½" ivory piece to each end. Make two of these units.

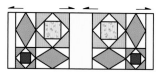

Make 2.

3. Sew the units from step 2 to the sides of the center square. Press toward the center square.

4. Piece a row of four Flower blocks, two 1½" x 7½" ivory pieces, and a 3½" x 7½" ivory piece together as shown. Make two of these rows and sew to the top and bottom of the quilt.

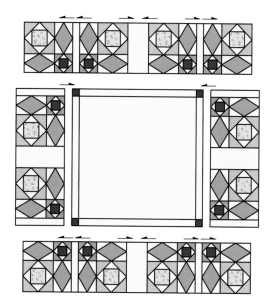

ADDING THE BORDERS

Refer to "Borders" on page 13. Measure the quilt through the center and cut the borders to fit.

1. Add the 2½" x 33½" ivory inner-border strips to the quilt sides. Add the 2½" x 37½" border strips to the top and bottom.

2. Sew the 10" x 37½" plaid outer-border strips to the sides of the quilt, followed by the 10" x 56½" strips to the top and bottom.

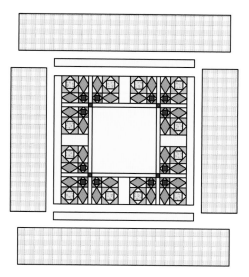

Decorating Hint

Use this quilt on a table and place a bouquet of coordinating flowers in the center.

FINISHING THE QUILT

1. Cut the backing fabric into two equal pieces and sew them together side by side to make a backing that is at least 4" larger than the quilt top.

2. Layer the backing, batting, and quilt top; baste the layers together.

3. Quilt as desired. The quilt shown was machine quilted. The Flower and Leaf blocks were stitched in the ditch. The center square was quilted with a grid of double lines, and in the plaid border, the quilting follows the lines in the fabric.

4. Referring to "Binding" on page 92, make and attach binding to your quilt.

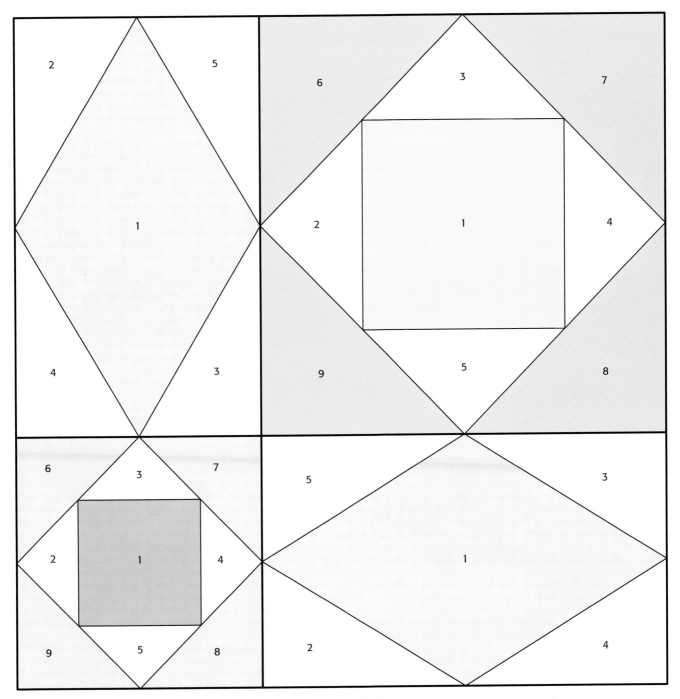

Petunia Block Foundation Pattern
Make 12.

Signs of Summer

Summer always seems to be too short. The flowers burst forth quickly, and the butterflies emerge, along with the mosquitoes! But enjoy watering the flowers and chasing the butterflies while you can, because winter is always just around the corner—in southern Manitoba anyway.

– Cori

Finished size: 14" x 9"

Appliquéd by Pearl Braun-Dyck; hand quilted by Cori Derksen.

MATERIALS

1 fat quarter of light lavender batik for background

Assorted scraps for watering can, flowers, leaves, and butterfly

1 fat quarter of fabric for backing

18" x 22" piece of batting

Embroidery floss: lavender, teal, and light green for *Summer,* antennae, and leaves

2 pairs of stretcher bars, 9" and 14" long

COMPLETING THE APPLIQUÉ AND EMBROIDERY

Refer to "Appliqué" on page 14 and "Embroidery Details" on page 15.

1. Trace the pattern on pages 50–51 onto the center of the batik fat quarter.

2. Cut your appliqué shapes and stitch them to the background. Work from the background to the foreground. Follow the numbers on the pattern; start with the watering can handle, the top of the handle, and then the top, middle, and bottom of the watering can. Stitch the spout last. Continue with the leaves, petals, and flower centers, followed by the back butterfly wings, top wing, and body.

3. Embroider the word *Summer* in lavender, the butterfly antennae in teal, and the veins of the leaves in light green.

FINISHING THE QUILT

1. Layer the backing, batting, and quilt top; baste the layers together.

2. Quilt as desired. We hand quilted around the appliqué shapes to outline and highlight them.

3. Refer to "Stretcher-Bar Framing" on page 94 to frame your quilt.

Connect to pattern on page 51.

Connect to pattern on page 50.

Dragonfly Baby Quilt

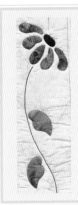

Designing a garden-theme baby quilt specifically for a boy was a bit of a challenge. The mud puddles quilt just didn't translate well! Then we thought of bugs and insects, which led to dragonflies—the perfect solution. This quilt, stitched in blocks of sherbet colors with whimsical dragonflies and flowers, will brighten up any baby's room.

– Cori

Finished quilt: 39" x 52"

MATERIALS

Yardage is based on 42"-wide fabric.

⅞ yard of medium blue for top and bottom border and binding

½ yard *each* of 6 fabrics: peach, yellow, light blue, green, lavender, and teal

⅛ yard or scraps of light green for leaves

⅛ yard or scraps of medium pink for flowers

⅛ yard or scraps of dark blue for dragonfly body

⅛ yard or scraps of medium blue for dragonfly wings

Scraps of dark pink for flower centers

2⅝ yards of fabric for backing*

43" x 56" piece of batting

Green embroidery floss for stems

> ** If your fabric is at least 42" wide after prewashing, 1¾ yards will be enough.*

Timesaving Option
For a great little summer wall hanging, reduce the pattern by 50%.

CUTTING

From the light blue fabric, cut:

❖ 2 squares, 7" x 7"
❖ 1 piece, 7" x 26½"

From the teal fabric, cut:

❖ 2 squares, 7" x 7"
❖ 1 piece 7" x 26½"

From the lavender fabric, cut:

❖ 1 piece, 7" x 13½"
❖ 1 piece, 7" x 26½"

From the yellow fabric, cut:

❖ 1 piece, 7" x 13½"
❖ 1 piece, 7" x 26½"

From the green fabric, cut:

❖ 1 piece, 7" x 13½"
❖ 1 piece, 7" x 26½"

From the peach fabric, cut:

❖ 1 piece, 7" x 13½"
❖ 1 piece, 7" x 26½"

From the medium blue fabric, cut:

❖ 2 pieces, 7" x 39½"
❖ 5 strips, 2½" x 42" (binding)

Pieced by Myra Harder; appliquéd by Pearl Braun-Dyck; quilted by Betty Klassen.

ASSEMBLING THE QUILT

Note: *We assembled the quilt before adding the appliqués. You can do the appliqué first if you prefer.*

1. Refer to the quilt diagram and assemble the quilt in vertical rows, beginning with row 1 on the left. Sew a 7" light blue square to each end of the 7" x 26½" teal piece. Press all seams toward the darker fabric.

2. For row 2, sew the 7" x 13½" lavender piece to the top of the 7" x 26½" yellow piece.

3. For row 3, sew the 7" x 26½" green piece to the top of the 7" x 13½" peach piece.

4. For row 4, sew 7" teal squares to the top and bottom of the 7" x 26½" lavender piece.

5. For row 5, sew the 7" x 13½" yellow piece to the top of the 7" x 26½" light blue piece.

6. For row 6, sew the 7" x 26½" peach piece to the top of the 7" x 13½" green piece.

7. Join the rows and press the seams in one direction.

8. Add medium blue 7" x 39½" pieces to the top and bottom of the quilt. Press toward the blue.

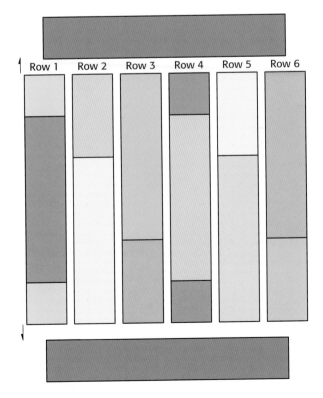

COMPLETING THE APPLIQUÉ AND EMBROIDERY

Refer to "Appliqué" on page 14 and "Embroidery Details" on page 15.

1. You will need four dragonflies, three flowers, and five leaves. Make freezer-paper templates from the appliqué patterns on page 56.

2. Referring to the photo for placement, appliqué the dragonfly wings and bodies, then the flower petals, centers, and leaves.

3. Embroider the flower stems.

Appliqué Advice

Have fun with the appliqués and add your own unique touch. We let a petal fall off one of the flowers for a touch of whimsy.

FINISHING THE QUILT

1. Cut the backing fabric into two equal pieces and sew them together side by side to make a backing that is 2" to 4" larger than the quilt top.

2. Layer the backing, batting, and quilt top; baste the layers together.

3. Quilt as desired. In the quilt shown, swirls were machine quilted to show the flight of the dragonflies. In the open areas, each block was outline quilted and filled with square grids. The blue borders were stitched with double parallel lines.

4. Referring to "Binding" on page 92, make and attach binding to your quilt.

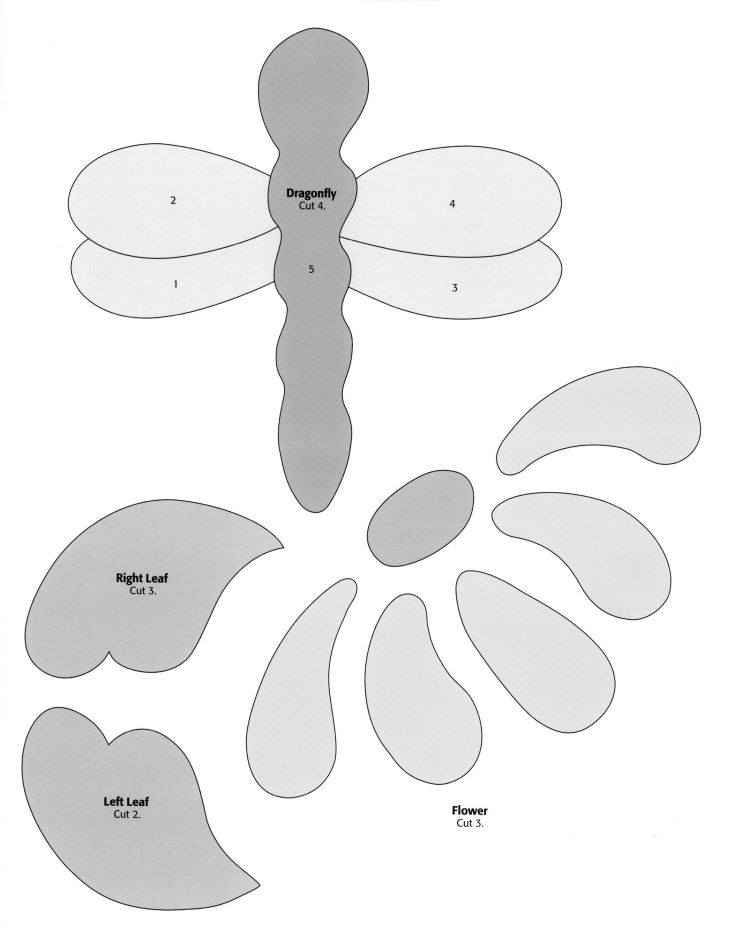

Dragonfly
Cut 4.

2

4

1

5

3

Right Leaf
Cut 3.

Left Leaf
Cut 2.

Flower
Cut 3.

(1) 4½ × 19

(2) 6 × 53½

(3) 6 × 13¾

Autumn

Autumn Joy

*Autumn sedum is one of those lovely fall garden surprises, and it is my
mother's favorite fall flower. When all the other flowers are withering away,
this foliage starts to bloom. For this quilt, the autumn color combination
of the floral print combined with pale orange, green, and purple seemed
perfect. It will add a warm accent to your home, while the flowers
outside add a wonderful spark to a fading fall garden.*

– Cori

Finished quilt: 68" x 68"

Finished block: 16" x 16"

MATERIALS

Yardage is based on 42"-wide fabric.

3¼ yards of yellow for background

2⅛ yards of floral print for setting triangles and
    binding

1⅛ yards of orange dot for paper-pieced blocks

1 yard of light orange for blocks

⅞ yard of purple for blocks

⅞ yard of green for paper-pieced blocks

4 yards of fabric for backing

72" x 72" piece of batting

CUTTING

From the yellow fabric, cut:

❖ 2 strips, 5" x 42"; crosscut into 52 pieces,
    1½" x 5"

❖ 3 strips, 10½" x 42"; crosscut into 52 pieces,
    2" x 10½"

❖ 3 strips, 2" x 42"; crosscut into 52 squares,
    2" x 2"

❖ 2 pieces, approximately 22" x 24"

From the purple fabric, cut:

❖ 13 squares, 1½" x 1½"

❖ 2 pieces, approximately 22" x 24"

From the light orange fabric, cut:

❖ 3 strips, 7½" x 42"; crosscut into 52 pieces,
    2" x 7½"

❖ 3 strips, 2" x 42"; crosscut into 52 squares,
    2" x 2"

From the floral print, cut:

❖ 2 squares, 24" x 24"; cut in half diagonally twice
    to make 8 quarter-square triangles

❖ 2 squares, 12¼" x 12¼"; cut in half diagonally
    once to make 4 half-square triangles

❖ 8 strips, 2½" x 42" (binding)

PAPER PIECING THE BLOCKS

1. Referring to "Paper Piecing" on page 11 and
   using the pattern on page 63, piece 52 blocks.

Make 52.

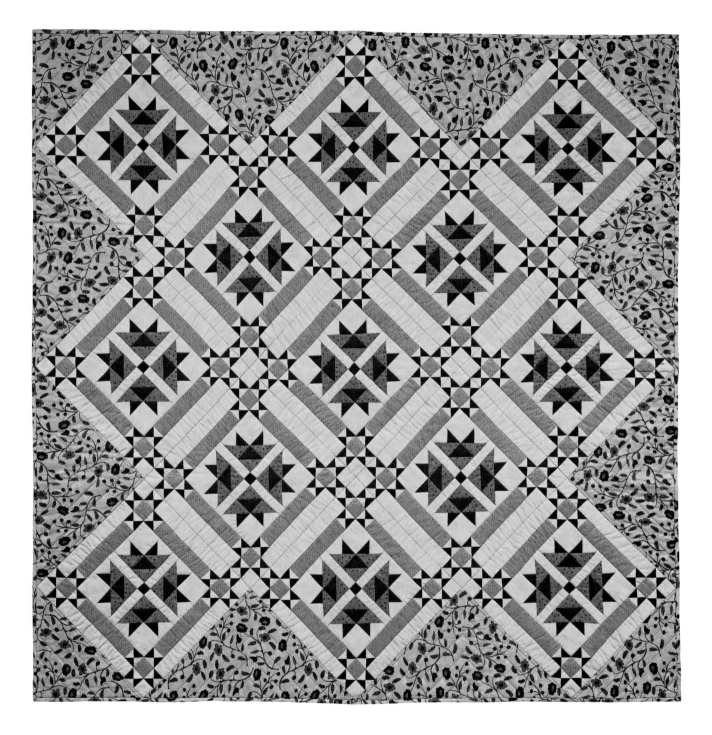

Pieced by Cori Derksen and Andrea Fehr; quilted by Betty Klassen.

2. Join two paper-pieced blocks with a 1½" x 5" yellow piece. Press toward the blocks. Make 26 units.

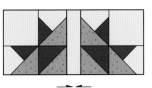

Make 26.

3. Sew a 1½" x 5" yellow piece to each side of a 1½" purple square. Press toward the purple. Use this piece as sashing between two units from step 2. Make 13 blocks.

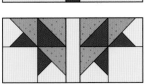

Make 13.

MAKING THE HOURGLASS BLOCKS

We used a technique called the grid method to piece the Hourglass blocks. It is the best way to accurately piece the 208 blocks that are needed.

Note: *You must sew with an accurate ¼"-wide seam allowance.*

1. On the wrong side of a 22" x 24" yellow piece, draw a 7 x 8 grid of 2¾" squares for a total of 56 squares.

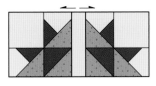

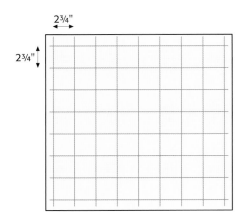

2. With right sides together, pin the marked yellow piece to a 22" x 24" purple piece.

3. Draw a diagonal grid over the first grid as shown. There will be a diagonal line through each square, alternating direction from square to square.

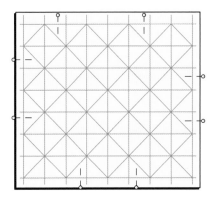

4. Sew exactly ¼" away from the diagonal lines on both sides.

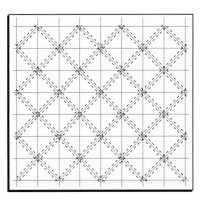

Stitch ¼" from diagonal lines.

5. Cut the units apart, using a rotary cutter and ruler, along the solid horizontal and vertical lines that you drew first. Press the seams toward the purple. There will be 112 half-square units. You need 104, so there will be some extra.

6. Repeat this process with the second pieces of yellow and purple fabrics so that you have a total of 208 half-square units.

7. Cut the units in half diagonally.

Cut 208.

8. Join the triangles to make the Hourglass blocks. Make 208.

Make 208.

9. Attach an Hourglass block to each end of a 2" x 7½" orange piece of fabric as shown, with the yellow of the Hourglass next to the orange fabric. Press toward the orange fabric. Make 52 units.

Make 52.

10. Sew one of the units from step 9 to each side of the pieced flower units. Press toward the step 9 unit.

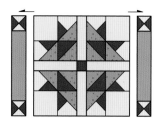

11. Add a 2" x 10½" yellow piece to each side of the units from step 10. Press toward the yellow.

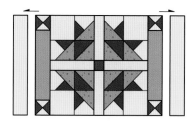

12. Sew an Hourglass block and a 2" orange square to each end of a unit from step 9 as shown. Make 26 of these units. Add one of these units to the top and bottom of each block.

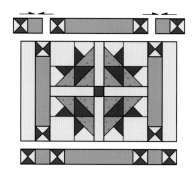

13. Sew an Hourglass block and a 2" yellow square to each end of a 2" x 10½" yellow piece as shown. Press toward the yellow. Make 26 of these units and sew to the top and bottom of each block. Make 13 blocks.

Make 13.

ASSEMBLING THE QUILT

Referring to the illustration at right, sew the blocks and floral setting triangles into diagonal rows. Press the seams in opposite directions from row to row. Sew the rows together.

FINISHING THE QUILT

1. Cut the backing fabric into two equal pieces and sew them together side by side to make a backing that is 4" larger than your quilt top.

2. Layer the backing, batting, and quilt top; baste the layers together.

3. Quilt as desired. The quilt shown was machine quilted by simply stitching in the ditch.

4. Referring to "Binding" on page 92, make and attach binding to your quilt.

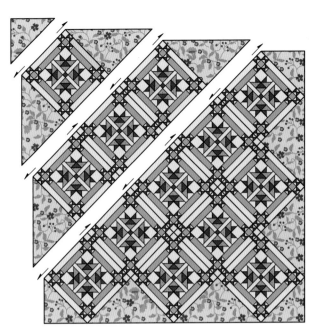

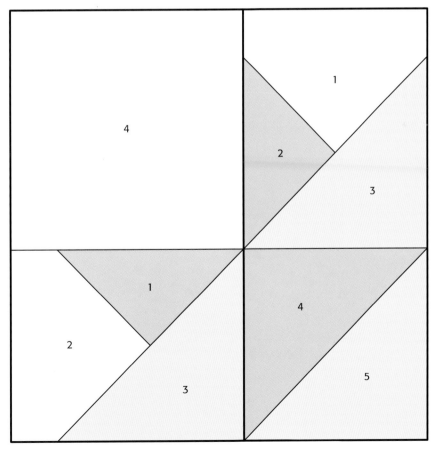

Autumn Joy Foundation Pattern
Make 52.

Signs of Autumn

Living in the country allows me to enjoy the many wondrous sights and sounds of autumn to the fullest. The pumpkins turn color and the harvest begins. Autumn also brings the celebration of Thanksgiving. Stitch up this autumn sign and welcome the harvest season in your own home.

– Cori

Finished quilt: 14" x 9"

Appliquéd by Pearl Braun-Dyck, hand quilted by Cori Derksen.

MATERIALS

1 fat quarter of tan batik for background

Scraps for pumpkins, leaves, and mice

1 fat quarter for backing

18" x 22" piece of batting

Embroidery floss: green, gray, and rust for stems, mouse details, and *Autumn*

2 pairs of stretcher bars, 9" and 14" long

COMPLETING THE APPLIQUÉ AND EMBROIDERY

Refer to "Appliqué" on page 14 and "Embroidery Details" on page 15.

1. Trace the pattern on pages 66–67 onto the middle of the batik fat quarter.

2. Starting from left to right and working from the background to the foreground, appliqué two small pumpkins and one large pumpkin, one medium and one small leaf, and two mice.

3. Embroider the stems in green. Embroider the mice tails, eyes, ears, and whiskers in gray. Embroider the word *Autumn* in rust.

FINISHING THE QUILT

1. Layer the backing, batting, and quilt top; baste the layers together.

2. Quilt as desired. The quilt shown was hand quilted, with the images and word outlined.

3. Refer to "Stretcher-Bar Framing" on page 94 to frame your quilt.

Connect to pattern on page 67.

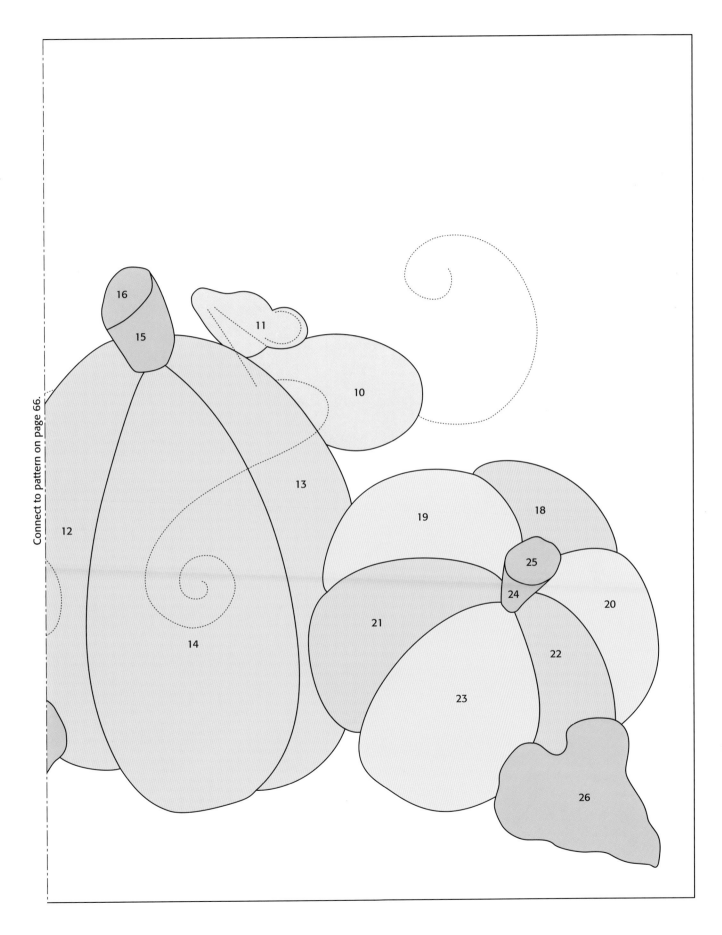

Connect to pattern on page 66.

Pumpkin Patch Baby Quilt

Fall is another favorite time of year for me. I love the colors, the smells, and the pumpkins! Every year come fall, my husband brings down a few straw bales from the hayloft for me, and we collect some corn shocks. My daughter Kierra likes to collect the pumpkins and gourds, and we make a fall display. This display then becomes a popular picture-taking spot. I also bring pumpkins indoors and display them with this quilt.

– Cori

Finished quilt: 35" x 42"

MATERIALS

Yardage is based on 42"-wide fabric.

1 yard of tan print for border and binding

½ yard of dark green for bias vines

½ yard or scraps for pumpkins

⅜ yard *each* of 4 different tan fabrics for background

Assorted scraps for leaves and mice

1⅜ yards of fabric for backing

39" x 46" piece of batting

Gray embroidery floss for mouse tail

CUTTING

Note: You may want to wait until the center of the quilt is complete before cutting borders.

From *each* of the 4 tan background fabrics, cut:

❧ 5 squares, 7½" x 7½"

From the tan print, cut:

❧ 4 strips, 4" x 35½" (borders)
❧ 5 strips, 2½" x 42" (binding)

From the dark green fabric, cut:

❧ 1¼"-wide bias strips to total approximately 165"

ASSEMBLING THE QUILT

1. Arrange the tan squares in five rows of four squares each, referring to the quilt diagram for placement.

2. Sew the squares together in rows. Press the seams in opposite directions from row to row.

3. Sew the rows together and press all the seams in the same direction.

4. Refer to "Borders" on page 13. Add the side borders, followed by the top and bottom borders. Press toward the borders.

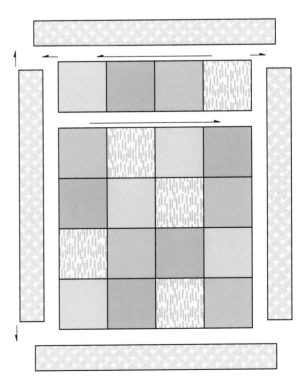

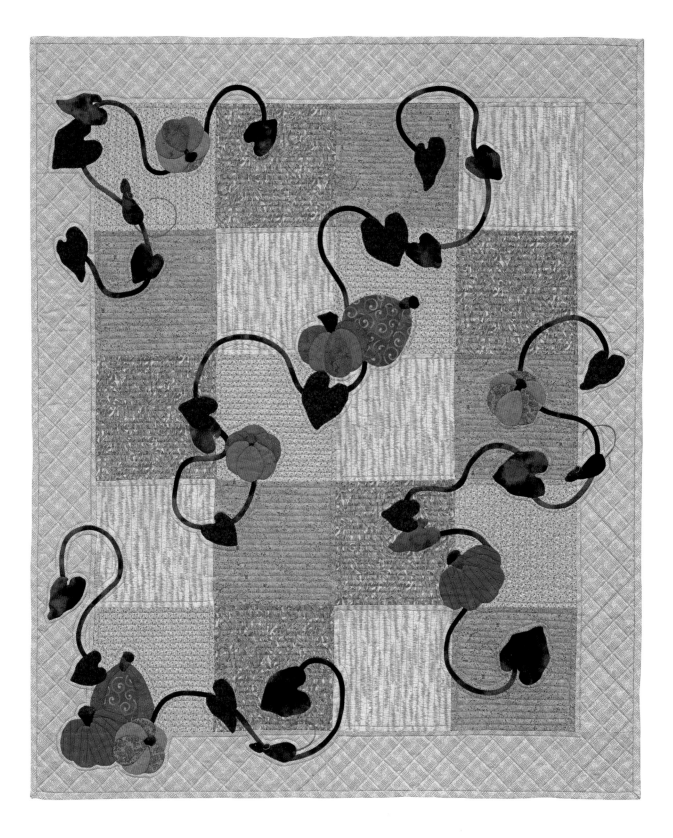

Pieced by Myra Harder; appliquéd by Pearl Braun-Dyck; quilted by Betty Klassen.

COMPLETING THE APPLIQUÉ AND EMBROIDERY

Refer to "Appliqué" and "Bias Tubes" on page 14, and "Embroidery Details" on page 15. Use the photograph on page 70 as a guide for placement. Always start appliquéing in the background and work your way to the foreground. For this quilt, begin with the vines, then add the leaves, mice, pumpkins, and stems.

1. Make freezer-paper templates by tracing the appliqué patterns on page 72.

2. Appliqué the upper-left group. You will need: 34" of ¼" dark green bias tube, one large leaf, two medium leaves, two small leaves, one small pumpkin, and one mouse.

Appliqué Advice

For smooth curves and easier stitching, pin and then baste the bias tubes in place before appliquéing.

3. Appliqué the center group. You will need 63" of ¼" dark green bias tube, two large leaves, two medium leaves, four small leaves, one large pumpkin, one medium pumpkin, and one small pumpkin.

4. Appliqué the right-side group. You will need: 48" of ¼" dark green bias tube, two large leaves, two medium leaves, one small leaf, one medium pumpkin, one small pumpkin, and one mouse.

5. Appliqué the lower-left group. You will need: 19" of ¼" dark green bias tube, one large leaf, two medium leaves, one small leaf, one large pumpkin, one medium pumpkin, one small pumpkin, and one mouse.

6. Embroider a tail on each mouse.

FINISHING THE QUILT

1. Layer the backing, batting, and quilt top; baste the layers together.

2. Quilt as desired. The quilt shown was machine quilted. The background squares were quilted with a repeating pattern of vertical and horizontal lines, then the vines, leaves, pumpkins, and mice were outline quilted ¼" away from the images. The border was quilted in a diagonal grid.

3. Referring to "Binding" on page 92, make and attach binding to your quilt.

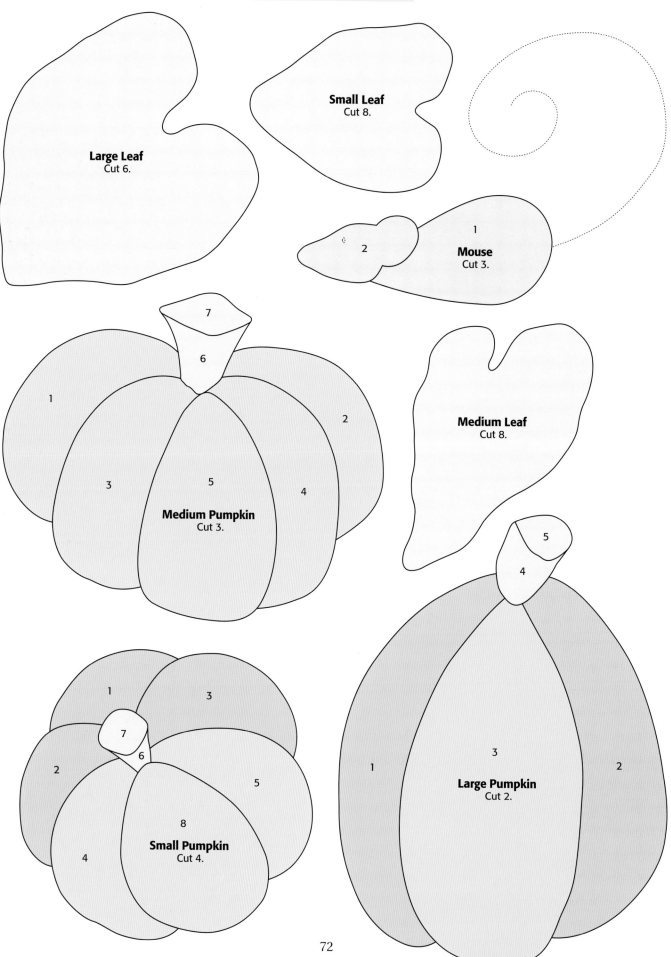

Large Leaf
Cut 6.

Small Leaf
Cut 8.

Mouse
Cut 3.

1

2

7

6

1

2

3

5

4

Medium Pumpkin
Cut 3.

Medium Leaf
Cut 8.

5

4

1

3

2

Large Pumpkin
Cut 2.

1

3

7

6

2

5

8

4

Small Pumpkin
Cut 4.

WINTER

Christmas Goose

This quilt features the block called Goose in the Pond. We designed this on paper many years ago but just never found the perfect fabrics. We finally found a wonderful red floral print that we both loved for the sashing and borders. Adding the greens to the blocks gave it a Christmas feel. You could also substitute golds for the greens to make a summery garden quilt. This quilt top is fast and easy to piece together! Use it as a wall hanging for a Christmas focal point, layer it on a guest bed, or use it as a table topper.

– Myra and Cori

Finished quilt: 71" x 71"

Finished block: 15" x 15"

MATERIALS

Yardage is based on 42"-wide fabric.

2⅝ yards of red print for sashing and borders

2⅛ yards of light green for Nine Patch sashing blocks

1⅛ yards of dark green for blocks and binding

¾ yard of cream for blocks

⅝ yard of red for blocks

⅝ yard of bright green for block centers and Nine Patch sashing blocks

4¼ yards of fabric for backing

75" x 75" piece of batting

CUTTING

From the cream fabric, cut:

❖ 15 strips, 1½" x 42"

From the red fabric for blocks, cut:

❖ 12 strips, 1½" x 42"

From the bright green fabric, cut:

❖ 2 strips, 3½" x 42"
❖ 5 strips, 1½" x 42"

From the lengthwise grain of the light green fabric, cut:

❖ 2 strips, 1½" x 59½" (inner-border top and bottom)
❖ 2 strips, 1½" x 57½" (inner-border sides)

From the remainder of the light green fabric, cut:

❖ 4 strips, 1½" x 42"
❖ 72 squares, 3½" x 3½"
❖ 36 squares, 3⅞" x 3⅞"; cut in half diagonally to make 72 half-square triangles

From the dark green fabric, cut:

❖ 4 strips, 3⅞" x 42". Cut into 36 squares, 3⅞" x 3⅞"; cut in half diagonally to make 72 half-square triangles
❖ 8 strips, 2½" x 42" (binding)

From the lengthwise grain of the red print, cut:

❖ 2 strips, 6½" x 71½" (outer-border top and bottom)
❖ 2 strips, 6½" x 59½" (outer-border sides)
❖ 24 pieces, 3½" x 15½"

Pieced by Myra Harder; quilted by Betty Klassen.

MAKING THE BLOCKS

1. Sew a red strip to each long side of a cream strip to make a strip set. Make three. Press toward the red strips. Crosscut the strip sets into a total of 72 units, 1½" wide.

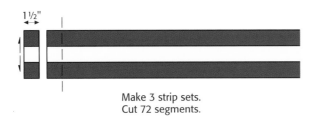

1½"

Make 3 strip sets.
Cut 72 segments.

2. Sew a cream strip to each long side of a red strip to make a strip set. Make two. Press toward the red strip. Crosscut the strip sets into a total of 36 units, 1½" wide.

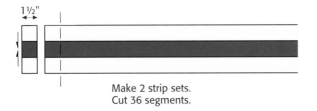

1½"

Make 2 strip sets.
Cut 36 segments.

3. Sew the units together to make 36 Nine Patch blocks.

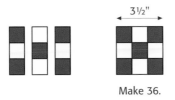

3½"

Make 36.

4. Sew a cream strip to each long side of a red strip to make a strip set. Make two. Press toward the red strip. Crosscut the strip sets into a total of 18 units, 3½" wide.

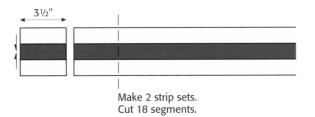

3½"

Make 2 strip sets.
Cut 18 segments.

5. Join two Nine Patch blocks to each end of the horizontal pieces. Press toward the Nine Patch blocks.

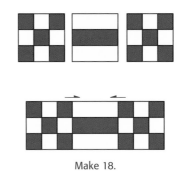

Make 18.

6. Sew the following strips together as shown: four cream strips, two red strips, and a 3½"-wide bright green strip. Press. Crosscut this strip set into 9 units, 3½" wide.

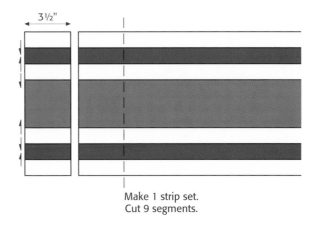

3½"

Make 1 strip set.
Cut 9 segments.

7. Join a Nine Patch unit from step 5 to each side of a unit from step 6 to form the center of the blocks. Make 9 block centers.

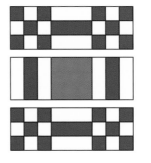
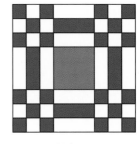

Make 9.

8. Join the light green half-square triangles to the dark green half-square triangles to form a unit. Press toward the dark green. Repeat to make 72.

Make 72.

9. Sew a half-square-triangle unit from step 8 to opposite sides of the light green 3½" squares. Press toward the light green squares. Repeat to make 36 of these units. Then sew one of these units to each side of the center blocks. Press.

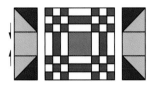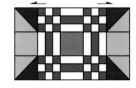

10. Sew a light green 3½" square to each end of the remaining half-square-triangle units from step 9. Press toward the light green squares. You should have 18 units.

Make 18.

11. Sew the units from step 10 to the top and bottom of the units from step 9 to make 9 blocks.

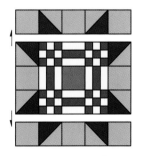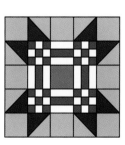

Make 9.

MAKING THE SASHING BLOCKS

1. Sew a 1½"-wide bright green strip on each side of a 1½"-wide light green strip to make a strip set. Make two. Press toward the bright green. Crosscut a total of 32 units, 1½" wide.

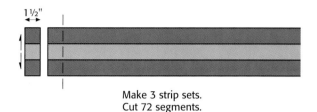

Make 3 strip sets.
Cut 72 segments.

2. Sew a light green 1½"-wide strip on each side of a bright green 1½"-wide strip to make a strip set. Press toward the bright green. Crosscut 16 units, 1½" wide.

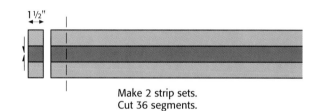

Make 2 strip sets.
Cut 36 segments.

3. Sew the units from step 1 and 2 together to form the 16 Nine Patch blocks for the sashing.

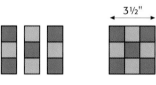

Make 16.

ASSEMBLING THE QUILT

1. The quilt is assembled in horizontal rows of blocks and sashing strips. Make the sashing and Nine Patch rows by sewing four green Nine Patch blocks and three red print 3½" x 15½" strips together. Press toward the sashing strips. Make four of these rows.

Make 4.

2. Sew together three large blocks and four red print 3½" x 15½" strips as shown. Press toward the sashing strips. Make three rows.

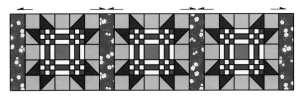

Make 3.

3. Sew the block rows and sashing rows together to make the quilt top. Press.

4. Refer to "Borders" on page 13. Add the light green inner side borders to the quilt, followed by the inner top and bottom borders. Press.

5. Add the red print outer side borders to the quilt, followed by the outer top and bottom borders. Press.

FINISHING THE QUILT

1. Cut the backing fabric into two equal pieces and sew them together to make a backing that is at least 4" larger than your quilt top.

2. Layer the backing, batting, and quilt top; baste the layers together.

3. Quilt as desired. The quilt shown was machine quilted with outline quilting ¼" away from all the seams in the blocks. The sashing and borders were quilted with parallel lines.

4. Referring to "Binding" on page 92, make and attach binding to your quilt.

Holly and Berries
Table Runner

I always have good intentions to make Christmas wall hangings or table toppers as gifts for the holidays, but it seems I never start early enough. This little table runner is quick to make and very festive. Crazy Patch blocks in shades of white and cream add a touch of vintage elegance to accompany the more modern version of holly and berries. Start this early enough, and you can make one for a gift and one for yourself!

– Cori

Finished quilt: 16" x 38"
Finished Crazy Patch block: 4" x 4"

MATERIALS

Yardage is based on 42"-wide fabric.

1 yard *total* of assorted light scraps for Crazy Patch blocks

⅜ yard of red stripe for outer border

⅜ yard of light tan for background

⅛ yard of green for inner border and holly leaves

Scraps of red for berries

⅝ yard of fabric for backing

⅜ yard of red for binding

20" x 42" piece of batting

Dark green embroidery floss for leaves

CUTTING

From the red stripe, cut:

❖ 2 pieces, 6½" x 16½"

From the green fabric, cut:

❖ 2 strips, 1½" x 16½"

From the light tan fabric, cut:

❖ 2 pieces, 6½" x 16½"

From the red fabric for binding, cut:

❖ 3 strips, 2½" x 42"

81

Pieced by Cori Derksen; appliquéd, embroidered, and quilted by Betty Klassen.

PAPER PIECING THE CRAZY PATCH BLOCKS

Using the assorted light fabrics, paper piece 12 Crazy Patch blocks; make six each of the two block patterns on page 84. Refer to "Paper Piecing" on page 11.

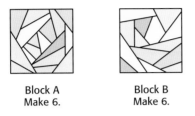

Block A
Make 6.

Block B
Make 6.

ASSEMBLING THE QUILT

Note: We assembled the quilt before adding the appliqués. You can do the appliqué first if you prefer.

1. Sew the Crazy Patch blocks into three rows of four blocks each.

2. Sew the border pieces, the Crazy Patch rows, and the light tan background pieces together as shown. Press.

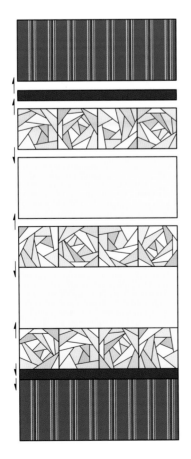

COMPLETING THE APPLIQUÉ AND EMBROIDERY

Refer to "Appliqué" on page 14 and "Embroidery Details" on page 15.

1. Trace the appliqué and embroidery patterns on pages 85–86 onto the light tan pieces.

2. Appliqué the berries and leaves.

3. Embroider the stem and veins of the leaves.

Take It Along

The embroidery and appliqué panels in this table runner make the perfect take-along project to work on whenever you're waiting or traveling, or when you have a few minutes to stitch by hand.

FINISHING THE QUILT

1. Layer the backing, batting, and quilt top; baste the layers together.

2. Quilt as desired. In our quilt, the Crazy Patch blocks were machine quilted in the ditch. The holly, berries, and embroidered stem were echo quilted by hand ¼" all around to create a textured effect. In the red striped border, the quilting follows the stripe.

3. Referring to "Binding" on page 92, make and attach binding to your quilt.

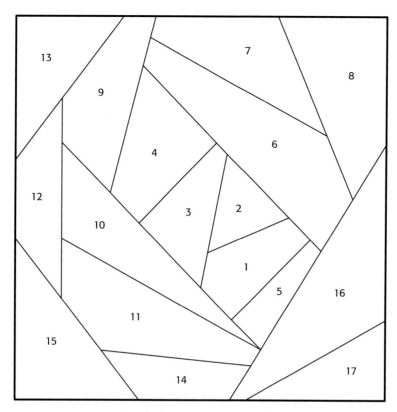

Crazy Patch Block A Foundation Pattern
Make 6.

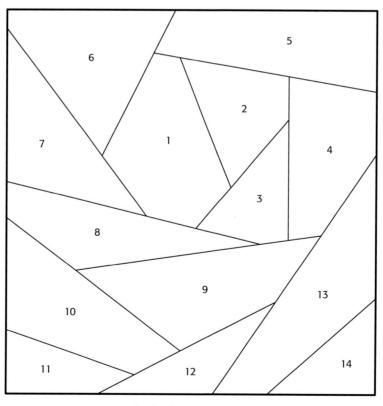

Crazy Patch Block B Foundation Pattern
Make 6.

Connect to pattern on page 86.

Connect to pattern on page 85.

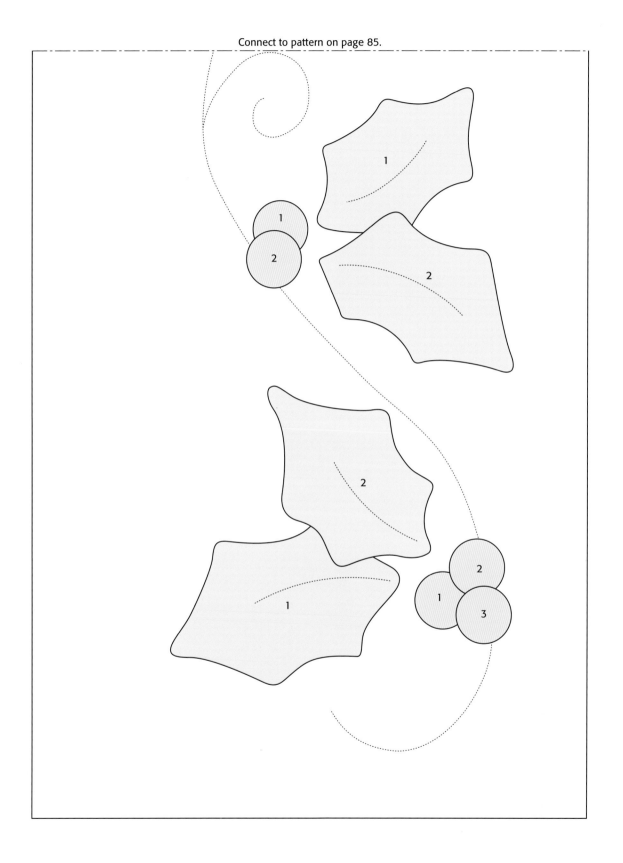

Signs of Winter

My mother loves the Canadian winters. She enjoys feeding the birds, and
her yard and gardens are as beautiful in winter as they are in other seasons.
This peaceful birdhouse scene was inspired as I walked out of the back
of her house and through her garden this past winter. Her garden was
filled with snow-covered branches and many empty birdhouses.

– Myra

Finished size: 14" x 9"

Appliquéd by Pearl Braun-Dyck; hand quilted by Cori Derksen.

COMPLETING THE APPLIQUÉ AND EMBROIDERY

Refer to "Appliqué" on page 14 and "Embroidery Details" on page 15.

1. Trace the appliqué pattern on pages 89 and 90 onto the middle of the batik fat quarter.

2. Appliqué the designs in the numbered order indicated on the pattern.

3. Embroider the snow line on the roof in white and the word *Winter* in blue in the lower-right corner.

MATERIALS

1 fat quarter of light blue batik for background

Assorted scraps for branch, snow, birdhouse, and roof

1 fat quarter for backing

18" x 22" piece of batting

Embroidery floss: white and blue for snow line and *Winter*

2 pairs of stretcher bars, 9" and 14" long

FINISHING THE QUILT

1. Layer the backing, batting, and quilt top; baste the layers together.

2. Quilt as desired. In the quilt shown, all of the images were outline quilted.

3. Refer to "Stretcher-Bar Framing" on page 94 to frame your quilt.

Connect to pattern on page 90.

Connect to pattern on page 89.

Finishing Techniques

It's always a good feeling when the quilt top is completed. The end is certainly in sight, but there are still several steps to take before it becomes a cozy and comfy quilt. If you haven't already decided how you are going to quilt your project, do so now. You can follow the seams and stitch in the ditch, try freehand quilting, or you could mark your quilt top with a quilting stencil or other design. Most quilters find it easiest to mark the top before layering and basting.

ASSEMBLING THE LAYERS

Before quilting, you will need to layer the top with the batting and backing.

1. Cut the backing and batting 4" to 6" larger than the pieced top. This will give you 2" to 3" extra on each side for any take-up that occurs during quilting. The instructions for each project in this book include the size to cut the batting and backing. For backings that have been pieced together, you may need to trim some of the excess away before continuing the process.

2. Place the backing, right side down, on a flat surface. Using masking tape, secure it in several places along the edges. Make sure the backing is smooth and taut. Position the batting over the backing and smooth it into place. Center the pieced top, right side up, over the batting and backing.

3. Working from the center out, baste the layers together. Use thread if you plan to hand quilt,

safety pins if you are going to machine quilt. Space pins or basting stitches 4" to 6" apart.

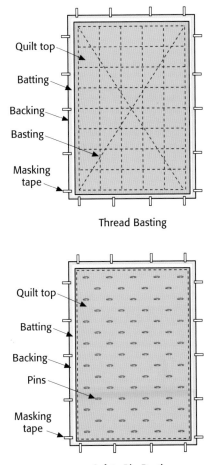

Thread Basting

Safety-Pin Basting

QUILTING

Quilting is an important finishing step. Not only does it hold the layers together but it also enhances the quilt pattern and adds dimension to the project. We love hand quilting; it adds to a quilt's value—both the monetary value and the heirloom quality as well.

Not everyone has the time for or the love of hand quilting, so machine quilting is another option. Machine quilting can be faster and allows you to make intricate patterns or repeating patterns easily. It is a good choice for quilts that will be heavily used or laundered often. The projects in this book illustrate both hand- and machine-quilting techniques and sometimes a combination of the two is also used.

ADDING A HANGING SLEEVE

We like to add a hanging sleeve to the back of our projects before we bind the quilt. It saves on hand stitching and results in a neater-looking finish on the back.

1. Cut a strip of fabric that is 6" wide with a length that is 1" less than the width of the finished project.

2. Press each end of the strip under ¼" and stitch in place.

3. Fold the strip in half lengthwise, wrong sides together. Baste the raw edges together to form a tube.

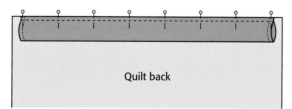

4. Center the raw edge of the strip along the top edge of the quilt back. Pin the sleeve in place.

Quilt back

5. Bind the quilt as instructed in the directions that follow, securing the sleeve in the seam.

6. After the binding is folded to the back and hand stitched in place, slipstitch the bottom of the sleeve to the quilt backing. Be careful not to stitch through to the front of the quilt.

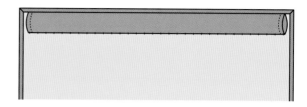

BINDING

Binding is the most common way to finish the edges of quilts. We use double-fold binding—the binding strip is folded in half before being stitched onto the edges. It is an easy and secure way to finish your project.

1. Cut the required number of strips as instructed for the project. Cut the strips across the width of the fabric.

2. Stitch the strips together on the diagonal to make one length that is long enough to go around your project. Place two strips right sides together so they are perpendicular to each other as shown. Draw a diagonal line on the top strip that extends from the point where the upper edges meet to the opposite point where the lower edges meet. Stitch along this line.

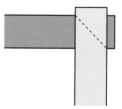

3. Trim the seam allowance to ¼". Press the seam allowance open. Add the remaining strips in the same manner.

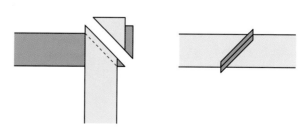

4. When all of the strips have been added, cut one end at a 45° angle. This will be the beginning of the strip. Press the binding in half lengthwise, wrong sides together, aligning the raw edges.

5. Beginning with the angled end, place the binding strip along one edge of the right side of the quilt top. Starting several inches away from a corner, align the raw edges. Leaving the first 8" of the binding unstitched, stitch the binding to the quilt. Use a ¼" seam allowance. Stop stitching ¼" from the corner. Backstitch and remove the quilt from the machine.

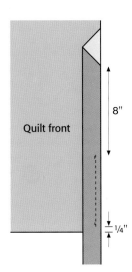

Quilt front

8"

¼"

6. Turn the project so you are ready to sew the next side. Fold the binding up so it creates a 45° angle fold.

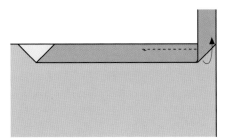

7. Place your finger on the fold to keep it in place; then fold the binding back down so the new fold is even with the top edge of the quilt and the raw edge of the binding is aligned with the side of the quilt. Beginning at the edge, stitch the binding to the quilt, stopping ¼" from the next corner. Repeat the folding and stitching process for each corner.

8. When you are 8" to 12" away from your starting point, stop stitching and remove the quilt from the machine. Cut the end of the binding strip so it overlaps the beginning of the binding strip by at least 5". Pin the ends together 3½" from the starting point. Clip the binding raw edges at the pin, being careful not to cut past the seam allowance or into the quilt layers. Open up the binding and match the clipped edges as shown, with right sides together. Stitch the binding strips together on the diagonal.

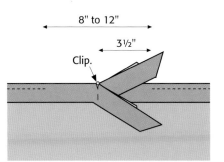

8" to 12"

3½"

Clip.

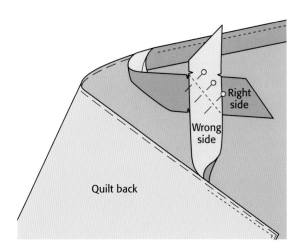

Right side

Wrong side

Quilt back

9. Refold the binding and check to make sure it fits the quilt. Trim the binding ends to ¼". Finish stitching the binding to the edge.

10. Fold the binding over the raw edges to the back of the quilt. Slipstitch the binding to the backing along the fold, mitering the corners.

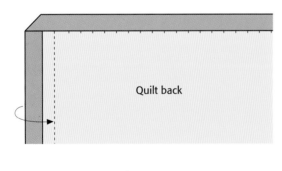

Quilt back

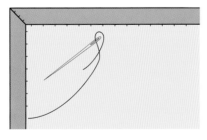

BLOCKING

We usually block all of our finished quilts to ensure that they lie perfectly flat and look their best.

1. Heavily mist your project from both sides and smooth out with your hand. If the quilt is not square, you can gently stretch and pin it to square it up.

2. Brush the entire project with a lint brush. This removes any stray threads or fuzz and helps to smooth out small creases.

3. Lay the quilt flat to dry.

STRETCHER-BAR FRAMING

To frame a quilted "sign" with stretcher bars, you will need a wooden frame cut to the desired finished size of your piece. We have ours made from 1" x 1" pine boards. Pine is a good choice because it is soft for easy stapling. We have the corners mitered and the front edge cut at an angle to produce a crisp edge. Anyone with basic carpentry tools can build this simple wooden frame.

An alternative would be to use artist's stretcher bars, available at art-supply stores. They are sold in pairs by length, so you will need to buy one pair equal to the width of your quilt and one pair equal to the length of your quilt. If the artist's stretcher bars don't come in the dimensions you need, you may need to add a border to make your quilt the right size.

1. Lay the quilted piece face down on a flat surface. Place the wooden frame, front edge down, in position on the quilted piece.

2. Mark the center along each edge of the quilt and mark the center on each side of the frame. Matching center points, wrap the backing fabric around the edges of the frame and staple in place. Wrap the batting and quilt top around the edges of the frame and staple in place at the centers. The piece should feel tight, yet not so tight that the quilting is pulled flat.

3. Continue stapling along the edges, from the centers out to about 3" from the corners. Staple the backing first and then the batting and quilt top. Stretch the piece as you go. Place the staples close enough together in both the backing and quilt top to avoid ripples in the fabrics.

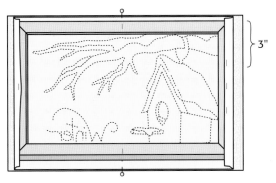

Staple backing at the center of all four sides; then staple to about 3" from the corners.

4. Trim the batting at the corners to eliminate bulk. Fold a 45° pleat to the inside to create a smooth corner. Staple in place. Continue stapling the backing, batting, and quilt top in place around the corners.

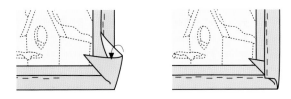

5. Trim excess fabric and batting close to the staples.

6. Add a picture hanger at the top center of the stretcher-bar frame.

SIGNING YOUR QUILT

Your quilt is not finished unless it is signed. You may think this is an unnecessary step, but you will thank yourself for it later, as will family members or others who receive quilts as gifts. You will need a permanent fabric-marking pen to include the following information on the label.

❖ Made by _____

❖ Hometown

❖ Date started and completed

❖ Any special occasion or reason for making the quilt

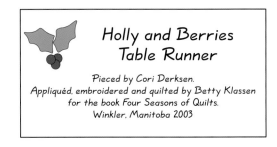

*Holly and Berries
Table Runner*

*Pieced by Cori Derksen.
Appliquéd, embroidered and quilted by Betty Klassen
for the book Four Seasons of Quilts.
Winkler, Manitoba 2003*

Now your quilt is finished!

Meet the Authors

Myra Harder and Cori Derksen

We began our design careers by wholesaling patterns and publishing two quilts in *American Patchwork and Quilting,* and now here we are four years and four books later! As stay-at-home moms, we feel fortunate that we can pursue careers and still be home raising our children. We've been friends for twenty-five years and each understands how the other thinks to the point that we can finish each other's sentences. This friendship has grown into a unique and successful partnership. During the past four years we've ventured out to speak to fellow quilters, present our trunk show, and teach classes. These opportunities have taught and inspired us and allowed us to make new friends.

Our other books include *Down in the Valley: Paper-Pieced Houses and Buildings, All through the Woods,* and *Traditional Quilts to Paper Piece.*

MYRA HARDER

My husband, Mark, and I live with our children, Samson and Robyn, in the small city of Winkler, in southern Manitoba, Canada. Most of our time is spent running after our children or having fun with friends down at the lake. Art and design have always been a part of my lifestyle, and now I use this background to make quilts so that future generations of our family will have something made by me.

CORI DERKSEN

I live on acreage west of Winkler, Manitoba, Canada, with my husband Randy, daughter Kierra, and son Lane. We all enjoy the outdoors and working on the yard and in the gardens. This book and its designs reflect a part of our lifestyle. During the spring and summer I spend a lot of time gardening, nurturing God's wonderful creation. During the long winters I like to scrapbook and, of course, to quilt!